MAKE AN OFFER

MAKE AN OFFER

BREAK THROUGH ANALYSIS PARALYSIS & GRAB THE CONFIDENCE YOU NEED TO BECOME A REAL ESTATE INVESTOR

JAY HELMS

Make an Offer

Although the author and publisher have made every effort to ensure that the information in this book was correct at press time, the author and publisher do not assume and hereby disclaim any liability to any party for any loss, damage, or disruption caused by errors or omissions, whether such errors or omissions result from negligence, accident, or any other cause. Adherence to all applicable laws and regulations, including international, federal, state and local governing professional licensing, business practices, advertising, and all other aspects of doing business in the US, Canada or any other jurisdiction is the sole responsibility of the reader and consumer. Neither the author nor the publisher assumes any responsibility or liability whatsoever on behalf of the consumer or reader of this material. Any perceived slight of any individual or organization is purely unintentional. The resources in this book are provided for informational purposes only and should not be used to replace the specialized training and professional judgment of a health care or mental health care professional.

Neither the author nor the publisher can be held responsible for the use of the information provided within this book. Please always consult a trained professional before making any decision regarding treatment of yourself or others.

ISBN: 979-8-9853557-0-3

"The night before our first deal is a vivid memory. The sheer terror of launching into a new venture with a new partner kept me up all night and made me want to puke my guts out. Once we closed, the reality set in, and we went to work. Three months later, I experienced the same feelings closing on our second deal. You learn to deal with the uncertainty, and it turns into excitement once you've done it a few times! I still get nervous the night before each closing we have. That never goes away."

—Gino Barbaro, Co-founder of Jake & Gino, jakeandgino.com

"Imagine a roller coaster ride that drops you from mount Everest, crushes you to the deepest depths of the sea, twists fate and changes directions leaving you feeling sick to your stomach . . . but whose ending is the smooth, slow motion of serenity. This just about sums up what the last 48 hours of my life have been whilst closing my first deal. There were several times I wanted to give up. I actually almost did. But by some grace from God, I was able to focus on the end game and I stuck it out. I feel like I've grown so much just from this first deal. Now I'm ready for round two. Bring it!"

—Michael Beasley, Husband, Father of 4, Full-Time Nurse

"The victory and success that comes through perseverance and grit is unlike any other feeling. It is a reminder that success does not come easy—but in the end, you never want it to come easy, because the challenges and tribulations that you overcome to achieve success teach you so much along the way. Grinding through your low moments, make your high moments taste that much sweeter."

—Savannah Arroyo, Founder TheNetWorthNurse.com,
Co-founder of Willow Investment Group

"Don't be afraid to start small, for example by buying a single-family property or even turning your current home into a rental. Smaller deals will subject less of your capital to risk and will reduce potential losses from any mistakes you make. At the same time, they will provide a fantastic learning opportunity and a natural steppingstone to doing larger deals and growing your portfolio for years to come."

—Anton Ivanov, Founder & CEO, DealCheck.io

"The emotions I experienced leading up to closing our first deal was a whirlwind. I went from having all the confidence in the world knowing I would change our family tree through this investment, to freaking out about losing all our savings. I felt unqualified, yet strangely ready. So much was on the line, and I had to make it work. Either this was going to be the worst mistake I ever made, or it was going to be the best decision of my life. The ball was in my court- now to move!"

—Cindy Byler, Financially Independent School Teacher at 29
Co-Founder of Passive Patriots

"It all starts with faith . . . having faith in yourself and your abilities to achieve whatever it is you want to achieve. If you believe in yourself enough, nothing will stop you. If you lack faith, it usually comes from a lack of education, which you should ALWAYS continue, or allowing negative self-talk bury you. Just get out of your own head and call a friend, a coach, a mentor, a parent, etc. One phone call can, and often does, change the trajectory of your entire journey."

—Tim Kelly, VP of Education, ActiveDutyPassiveIncome.com

"I had heard that your first deal will never make you rich, but that it could get you started on your path to riches. I didn't quite believe it until I did my first deal. Fast forward a few years from doing my first deal and I truly believe getting your first deal done, any way possible, is one of the most important things when becoming a real estate investor."

—Robert Leonard, VP Growth & Innovation and Podcast Host
The Investor's Podcast Network

"Closing my first deal I ran the gamut of emotions from, "this will never work" and "are you buying at the right price?" To "I'm the best negotiator in town" and "let's do this again!" Pressing into the unknown and facing my fears are two of the greatest things I've learned on this journey to becoming an Entrepreneur and Real Estate Investor. I constantly think about the worst-case scenarios, accept them and then press on towards action."

—Todd Helzer, Owner BuyBhamHouses.com

"Right before getting under contract, I watched a video where a highly experienced investor said: *'It won't be a smooth ride. There will be a bunch of obstacles and bumps on the road. But it's ok. Something always goes wrong. It's ok, you will go through all of it.'* And I got so many of those challenges while trying to get my self-storage facility but none of them stopped me from closing. I remembered the voice: *'It's ok, you will surpass all those roadblocks.'* And I kept going until I got it close after 4.5 months of a bumpy road. And now I am a self-storage owner. I am a business owner and a commercial real estate investor."

—Masha Klapanova, Self-Storage Owner & Real Estate Investor
Top Choice Investment Group

"My first deal taught me one massively important thing that aspiring investors don't quite grasp until they experience it first-hand. You'll never be 100% ready for your first deal. You'll maybe be 50% ready at best. You need to just jump in and trust yourself to learn as you go. Not knowing forces you to focus only on what's ahead of you and block out the noise—which is usually the main driver of the dreaded analysis paralysis. Don't underestimate your ability to learn on your feet and make things happen, despite all odds!"

—Matt Porcaro, Founder The203kWay.com

A SPECIAL INVITATION

Readers and listeners of *Make an Offer* find additional support and inspiration by being around like-minded individuals, from all over the country, who are on their own real estate investing journey. Some are just beginning to look, while others have strapped on their boots and are trekking through their next deal. Regardless of where you are in your journey, I can guarantee that being around like-minded individuals will inspire, motivate, and propel you to overcome your next challenge. As a token of my appreciation for purchasing this book, I want to specially invite you to ***join an Ask Me Anything session. This free event is for folks just like YOU!***

Register for the next session @ **www.W2Capitalist.com/MakeAnOffer**

AUDIO BOOK VERSION

Grab a copy of the audiobook. Here is the link to do that: **www.W2Capitalist.com/MakeAnOffer**

BONUS CHAPTER

Sawyer and Hellen's journey doesn't stop at the end of this book. Find out what happens next in the
BONUS chapter that awaits at **www.W2Capitalist.com/MakeAnOffer**

WHAT'S THAT PHRASE MEAN?

Throughout this book, you may read terms or phrases that do not make sense to you or you just need more clarity on. Most of these are defined on the accompanying resource page at **www.W2Capitalist.com/MakeAnOffer,** but if there is a term or phrase you do not understand and cannot find the definition on **www.W2Capitalist.com/MakeAnOffer** site, then email me directly, **jay@w2capitalist.com**.

MY MISSION

It is my mission to help you build multiple active and passive income streams through real estate investing so you can achieve financial freedom and build legacy wealth. Building your portfolio starts with your hardest deal, your first deal. You don't know what you don't know, and this short book answers the who, what, when, why, and how to overcome the hardest part for beginner investors.

DEDICATION

This book is dedicated to my wife, Cassie, my son, Rowland, and my daughters, Stella and Ellen Anne. Without your love and support in the craziness we call life, this would not have been possible.

TABLE OF CONTENTS

INTRODUCTION

INTRODUCTION

Living paycheck to paycheck, being stagnant in your job growth, and lacking the courage to discover and take the next logical step to building wealth results in paralysis analysis.

This book is a little story about how people like you and me can find the confidence to shatter our analysis paralysis, eliminate our doubts and fears, and begin adding multiple streams of income by building a real estate investment portfolio while working a full-time job. Because the first one is always the hardest, this book is set up to help you close that first deal in a way that you can carry that momentum to closing the next one and then the next one and the next. Side hustling your way to building multiple streams of income through real estate investing will relieve the stress and anxiety that comes with financially accomplishing your goals.

The stigma that all real estate investors start super wealthy is *false*.

With a negative net worth and living paycheck to paycheck, I started conservatively investing in real estate in 2014. Six years later, I comfortably exited the W2 world to financial independence with over one million dollars in real estate assets.

Building multiple streams of income through real estate will remove the stress and anxiety of financially accomplishing your goals. You will no longer worry about being fired, acquired, or laid off. In fact, by offloading your financial burden to other multiple-income producing avenues, you will become a more focused employee, providing you with the flexibility and mental freedom to be more present with your family and friends. And all of this starts with making that first offer.

My promise to you: You're not alone. The fear, uncertainty, and doubt (FUD) you have about beginning your investing journey are *not* unique. What's rare are people who can muster up the courage to penetrate their FUD by themselves. But that's where this book comes in. You do not have to do it by yourself. With sound investing criteria and a proper support system, you'll instantly begin to build wealth, no longer be living paycheck to paycheck, and have the option to exit your W2 career in three–five years.

Andrew Carnegie is quoted as saying, "90 percent of all millionaires become so through owning real estate," and you can be the next one.

Having multiple streams of income starts with finding the confidence to take the most logical necessary steps to close on your first deal. You need to *Make an Offer*.

Listen, you've waited long enough to find the courage to start the rest of your life. Your wealthy-no-longer-scraping-to-get-by life filled with joy, happiness, and freedom like you've never experienced is waiting. Your time to begin your journey is now.

YOUR NEXT STEPS:

1. Read the next three chapters of this book today. Yes, right now even. The chapters in this book are extremely short and reading the first three will not take you long.
2. Go to **www.W2Capitalist.com/MakeAnOffer** and schedule your **free** *Ask Me Anything* session. This is an exclusive invite for folks just like you.

WHO THIS BOOK IS FOR:

- W2 employees and entrepreneurs
- Aspiring Real Estate investors
- Folks that suffer from analysis paralysis
- Realtors who want to invest
- Folks lacking the confidence to invest in their first Real Estate deal
- Real Estate investing skeptics
- Husbands, wives, and young parents who want to begin building generational wealth through Real Estate investing
- Experienced Real Estate investors lacking the confidence to transition asset types or strategies

WHO THIS BOOK IS *NOT* FOR:

- Experienced Real Estate investors who have the confidence it takes to grow
- The independently wealthy

THE FORMAT OF THIS BOOK:

At the end of each short chapter are action items. This is not homework but rather challenges for you to accomplish to begin your journey to becoming a real estate investor. No one will ask to make sure you did them, but consider them the guiding light, your next steps to making an offer that will put you on an expedited path to obtaining your first real estate investment property. You will notice that these are in checkbox list format. I'm a big checklist guy for two reasons: #1 to help me remember and #2 I love the dopamine hit my body produces when I'm able to check something off my list. Sometimes when my wife and I are at the grocery store, working our way up and down the aisles, if she grabs something that's not on our list, I'll write it down just so I get the pleasure of marking it off.

To grab a condensed version of the entire checklist, check out this book's resource page at **www.W2Capitalist.com/MakeAnOffer**

Having a portfolio of cash-producing assets will help eliminate the stress and anxiety that comes with living the life you've always dreamed about and deserve. This can be yours.

As Bob Seger sings, turn the page.

CHAPTER 1

THE BIG NEWS, THE ACQUISITION

"People who don't have goals work for people who do."

—Jack Canfield

CHAPTER 1

Meet Sawyer. Like you, he is a hard worker, is a devoted spouse, and has ambitions to forge his way to the top of the corporate ladder. Raised in a normal house in small-town USA, he graduated from a normal high school and a not-so-big university. Sawyer was an average student, but when it came to his professional accomplishments, he met challenges head-on and always excelled. However, in his six-foot-two, athletic frame, Sawyer awkwardly experienced and continues to experience confidence issues. It does not matter how hard he works, it does not matter how much formal education he puts himself through, it does not matter how many books he reads on building and fine-tuning his career, and it does not matter how many promotions he earns—he can't seem to pierce the barrier of living paycheck to paycheck.

On an exceptionally cold weekend in mid-January, Sawyer sits anxiously on the edge of their king-sized bed, waiting for his wife, Hellen, whom he had just married four months earlier, to come out of the bathroom with some potential news.

A little door handle jiggle, a crack of the door, then the sight of her beautiful face with an unmistakable grin . . .

"We're pregnant," Hellen immediately blurts out, with hands in the air, dancing a little jig.

"Are you serious?" Sawyer leaps to his bride, gives her the biggest hug he could squeeze out, kisses her on the lips, and slowly sits back down on their bed as reality starts to sink in . . . "Now what?"

***

Monday morning started out like any other day for Sawyer. He woke around 7:45, drug his butt slowly out of bed, went downstairs to their small white cabinet, granite countertop L-shaped kitchen, poured himself a glass of lukewarm water straight from the faucet, inhaled the water with a few big gulps, and immediately went back upstairs to his home office.

Sitting at his office desk, he thinks, *No client visits today; just admin and planning work.*

A few years ago, Sawyer and Hellen were allowed to move closer to his clients and work remotely from the corporate office. Since moving, Sawyer's workdays went one of two ways: (1) day trips, driving to visit happy clients, or (2) conference calls and admin work from his home office.

At 10:01 a.m., his phone rings: the boss.

"Hey. I need you up here next week. In your inbox is a non-disclosure agreement I need you to sign. We may have a buyer for the company, and I need you up here as part of their due diligence process."

"What? A buyer? Who is it? Why is the company for sale?" Sawyer quickly says.

"Look, I'll explain more next week. I'm taking the executive team to dinner Monday night to explain everything in more detail. Just be up here for that and plan to stay for a few days."

CHAPTER 1

"You got it, boss. I'll see you then." As Sawyer hangs up his phone, he sits back in his chair and thinks, *What the hell was that?*

It wasn't good.

Two months after discovering the exciting news of their first child on the way, Sawyer finds himself in the middle of an acquisition at work. As a principal of a startup IT company, Sawyer spent the better part of the last decade putting in long nights and weekends onboarding one customer after another, feeling like he was an owner of something that was going to be great, but those thoughts and feelings served as nothing but memories now as he and his coworkers found themselves being acquired and sucked up into a much larger organization. With this, he would go from being hired as principal employee number five and helping grow the company to over thirty employees, to now transitioning to a company with over three hundred employees. Changes were coming.

***

Four months have gone by since the acquisition was inked. New logos, new policies, new bosses, new rules.

"Hey, Sawyer, I hate to tell you this, but the board voted last night, and when our agreement comes up next month, we're not going to renew," says Frank from the other end of the phone.

"Not going to renew? But, Frank, you guys have been our customer, my customer, that I served for the last ten years. Last week when we met you made no hint that things were this bad, or bad in general. I apologize for my volume and scattered verbal-ness right now, but this comes as a complete shock to me. Help me understand."

"You're right, Sawyer. Things have been good but not great. You guys just aren't the same since the acquisition happened, and the board feels it's in our best interest to move on—"

"Wait! Move on? Move on to who?"

"I'll let you know next week. We've finalized it down to two companies, and I'll let you know so we can start the transition process."

"Transition process?" Sawyer questions as reality set in, and a cold sweat bubbles all over his body. Frank is Sawyer's biggest account, and the way the rest of the acquisition is going, Sawyer knows immediately this customer loss would surely get him fired. *Recently married, baby on the way, failing acquisition, and now fired?*

Frank speaks up. "Look, Sawyer, it's not personal; it's just business. The board feels that we are no longer a big fish in a little pond, and you have to admit, the service that we've received the last few months from your support staff, well, actually hasn't been stellar."

Sawyer sits there speechless as the reality of the situation continues to set in.

"Sawyer, can you hear me? Are you still there? . . . Sawyer?"

"Yes, Frank, I'm still here," Sawyer stutters. "Frank, I agree we are in this acquisition, and with things moving around, it has affected our support, but the last few months versus ten years of—"

"Sawyer, the board has voted. We're moving on. There isn't anything you can do at this point. There isn't anything I can do at this point. I'll call you next week to introduce you to our new vendor." Frank disconnects.

Unfortunately for Sawyer, that was the first of many calls he'd receive like that over the next several months. Hell, some clients wouldn't even offer a courteous call, they'd send an email, or even worse, a certified registered letter to the corporate office, and Sawyer would just find out from one of his coworkers or, typically, his new boss. Each time a client left, the pressure and anxiety over his job security and a new addition on the way weighed heavier and heavier and heavier. Of course, the surprise trips by his new boss, now his third new boss in as many months since the original acquisition, added to the growing stress and pressure as well. Something had to change.

At least, thanks to audiobooks, the hours Sawyer spent behind the steering wheel of his Toyota Camry every week were not mundane. Double win for Sawyer because he hated to physically read. Well, it's not that he hated physically reading books as much as he instantly would fall asleep every time he picked up a hard back or paper copy. Typically, he would yawn after the first few sentences, but the introduction of audiobooks changed the game for him. At times, Sawyer would listen to a book and become so deeply mentally connected that he'd snap to and realize he magically arrived at his first appointment . . . an hour and a half away! He is no longer stressed over being stuck in traffic, as that just meant more business education and personal development time for Sawyer.

***

By this time in his career, managing several teams and dozens and dozens of large clients, Sawyer had adopted a management concept he discovered in one of his audiobooks: *One instance is an anomaly. Two's a pattern. Third time is a trend. You pay attention to the patterns, but you manage the trends.*

Sawyer adopted this management philosophy into his personal life, so when he kept hearing the name of the book *Rich Dad Poor Dad*, he added it to his audio library, and it was today's choice on his commute to see clients.

"Everything the working class has been told to do; the rich do not do. That is my message," announces Kiyosaki, author of *Rich Dad Poor Dad*. "One dad had a habit of saying, 'I can't afford it.' The other dad forbade those words to be used. He insisted I ask, 'How can I afford it?' One is a statement, and the other is a question. One lets you off the hook, and the other forces you to think," continues Kiyosaki.

Pause. For the first time ever, Sawyer presses pause on his audiobook as those last few sentences echo in his brain.

"One is a statement; the other is a question. One lets you off the hook. The other forces you to think," Sawyer exclaims as he crosses the most brilliant epiphany bridge ever trekked.

CHAPTER 1

It was this excitement, the kind of heart-pounding excitement you feel with each thundering boom during the grand finale of a July 4th celebration, that must have made his foot heavier. He glances down. *Ninety-two miles per hour? Slow down, son.*

"Don't get any speeding tickets," Sawyer's dad typically told him when he called from the road.

His dad also used to say, "We can't afford that" a lot. *I never want to tell my kid(s) that we can't afford something but doing this job and barely getting by is never going to work. I must do something to get out of this rat race. What do wealthy people do to get wealthy?*

As Sawyer reflects on this, he realizes he is pulling into his home driveway. He had been deep in thought about what he just heard from Kiyosaki. *Another day of vising clients in the books,* he thought with a hint of relief and now excitement. Putting the car in park, he hurriedly grabs his belongings and rushes toward the front door, as if he were a man on a mission. Hellen greets him at the front door with a hug and a soft kiss on his lips as he slides his shoes off behind the front door. The house smells delicious as supper was almost ready.

"Is that fettuccini alfredo I smell?" he asks, setting up his laptop at the dining room table.

"Why yes, yes, it is."

"Great! I'm going to need to carb up," Sawyer jokes. "It's a working dinner tonight, hun. I have some very important research to do, tonight!"

This wasn't the typical ambition Sawyer arrived home with after visiting clients, especially after the acquisition. Hellen latches onto and is motivated by his excitement. "Oh yea? What's up, babe?!"

"Wealth. Wealth creation, that's what's up. We've been doing this all wrong," exclaims Sawyer as he runs upstairs to get changed for dinner.

Over dinner Hellen peers at her husband. "Ok, so what do we do?" she asks.

"I don't know, but that's what we're researching tonight."

Throughout the night and into the early morning hours, he conducts some research. After researching it, Sawyer concludes he and Hellen are meant to stay in the middle-class rat race and their future family has no shot of building real wealth. Every article, every post, everything he read pointed to people getting wealthy by owning real estate.

We can barely afford where we live now, so how can we even begin to think of buying something else? What the hell?! I guess we could slum it for a while in the hood and save up some money or move back in with Mom and Dad . . . neither of which he felt confident selling to his now five-month pregnant wife.

Feeling defeated, Sawyer retires for the night. Weeks go by and Sawyer falls back into his same old miserable routine: client visits, admin days, more clients upset because of "acquisition issues," more clients leaving, more pressure from his new boss, baby arriving soon. No matter how horrible his day would go, Sawyer could not get this whole thought of building wealth, building true wealth, out of his mind.

CHAPTER 1

There Sawyer sits, hunched over at his desk, head in hands, feeling the stress and anxiety bubbling up to his shoulders and thinks, *Why are you so afraid? What's your big deal, bro?*

He is a victim of the system. He had been trained since kindergarten to sit at a certain place until told to do something else and to stay in a building for a required amount of hours a day, only to have work sent home with him. The more these thoughts simmer in his head, the more upset and angrier he becomes.

***

"Hellen?" Sawyer questions as he sits on the floor in the baby's room, feeling lost as he cannot find the instructions to complete the next step in putting together the crib.

"Yes, my love?"

"Who do we know that invests in real estate? Who can I call?"

Hellen sits silently in deep thought but only for a moment. "Let's look it up."

"Look it up?"

"Yes, you said '90 percent of millionaires became that way through real estate investing,' so surely there's a group or club you can join. So, yea, let's look it up."

Putting a pause on the baby crib construction, Sawyer rushes off to snatch his laptop. Moments later he strolls back into the soon-to-be baby's room, balancing his laptop on one hand while single-handedly typing with the other and cautiously meandering through a landfill of instructions and parts.

Zoned into this screen, Sawyer sits back down on the floor and feverishly types with both hands. "Hun?"

"Yea, babe?"

"You're a genius! There are a couple of groups here in town that meet every month." But Sawyer's steam engine quickly came to a halt. Through his excitement, he forgot just how much he hated new people, how much he hated being in crowds, and how much he hated being the "new person" in the room that everyone would want to talk with.

***

YOUR NEXT STEPS TO MAKE AN OFFER:

- ☐ Visualization Exercise: Visualization is the formation of a mental scenario or image, a grey-matter flex game of "What Ifs." Spend five–ten minutes visualizing what your world would look like and how you would provide for yourself and/or your family if you received the call today that the company you worked for was being acquired and you were in imminent danger of being fired or laid off. How would you pay your bills? How would you afford the place you live? How would you still enjoy and afford to do the things you love? How would you find another job? Does this mean you're uprooting your family and moving to a different city, or a different state, or a different country even?
- ☐ Research: Google "[your city] real estate investor meetup" or "[your city] REIA," or "[your city] real estate investor association." I'll instruct you what to do with these results at the end of Chapter 2.
- ☐ Who Do You Know: Talk to just five people about your ambitions to explore real estate investing. Ask them who they know that already invests and ask for an introduction. Bonus credit, and highly suggested, buy them that round of coffee, beverage, or lunch.
- ☐ Proceed to Chapter 2.

CHAPTER 2

AN INTROVERT'S REALITY

"In the real estate business, you learn more about people, and you learn more about community issues, you learn more about life, you learn more about the impact of government, probably than any other profession that I know of."

—Johnny Isakson

CHAPTER 2

Sawyer and Hellen spent most Sunday evenings making homemade pizzas. As the aroma of Italian herbs and spices combined with melted mozzarella filled the air of their three-bed, two-bath home, Sawyer and Hellen relax on their synthetic upholstered couch, waiting for the timer to go off while watching reruns of *The Office*.

While he had a good forty-eight hours of freedom from the painful customer calls and meetings, by Sunday evening, Sawyer would experience a small glimpse of depression, for this freedom would soon end, and then it was back to the salt mine with bleeding, calloused hands. But he had to admit, watching the first-person anecdotal comedy experience that was his work life provided a nice relief. He would always tell Hellen, "I work for Michael Scott and the Dunder Mifflin paper company." Every Sunday night, he would tell Hellen events from his job and how it paralleled perfectly with tonight's episode he had seen a hundred times.

This Sunday is no different. When a beep pierces the air, Hellen glances at Sawyer, wondering what he is thinking about. It has to be something intense; otherwise, he never would have allowed the oven timer to go off. Sawyer hated the tone and sound of that timer so much that he would try to cancel it before it hit zero.

"Hun?" asks Hellen.

No response.

"Hun?" Hellen says again, slightly louder this time. Still, no response. *How can he not hear me; he's rubbing my feet.*

"Hello?! Earth to Sawyer. Come in, Sawyer. Over," Hellen says, as if she was playing the role of flight director at Mission Control Center in Houston.

"Yes? Yes, hun? Why are you screaming at me? And why is the oven timer going off?! God, I hate the sound of that!" He pushes Hellen's feet aside, gets up from the couch and starts stomping toward the kitchen.

"Because that was the third time I tried to get your attention. You had that gaze on your face. You know that glare where you're thinking about work when you shouldn't be because it's family time? You know that gawk I'm referring to, don't you? That stare you get right before you tell me that you're not hungry and you'll just demolish a bowl of cereal later. We both know you're hungry, you're just on the edge of depression because you're already thinking about work tomorrow. Aren't you?" Hellen joins her husband in the kitchen to check on the pizzas.

Turning off the oven timer, he says, "Yea, I know. It wasn't work that I was thinking of, though."

"Oh really? What was it then? Was it meeee?" Hellen gushes as she leans in with heart-shaped hands extended in front of her face.

With a chuckle and a grin, Sawyer replies, "Yes, babe. It was you."

"Ooook, seriously, what was it?"

CHAPTER 2

"I don't know. I just—"

"You just love me so much that you don't know what to do with yourself sometimes? Do I blow your mind?"

Hellen has this sense of knowing when he is stressing over something, typically his job or what he feels is a lack of financial success. Best to be playful and distract him from those depressing thoughts and onto something more enjoyable. Although she knows Sawyer is aware that this is what she is doing, after all, they had done this dance many, many times before—almost every Sunday evening since the acquisition—she continues with the tactic anyway.

Lightning up a bit, Sawyer says, "Yes, babe. You blow my mind and my—"

"Hey! So, what were you really thinking about? If it wasn't work, what were you thinking about?" Hellen asks.

"I was thinking about going to the next REIA meeting."

"Oh yea? Well, that sounds interesting, but why are you thinking so hard and getting depressed over going to a meeting?"

"I don't know, babe. You know I don't like crowds, big or small, especially when I feel like I'll be the center of attention. And at this meeting, I will be the guy in a room full of weirdos I don't know. I don't want that. And what if someone talks to me?"

"What IF someone talks to you? Well, I guess that'll be great, won't it? Can you grab us some plates?" Hellen slices up the homemade deliciousness, whose delightful aroma is spreading throughout their home.

"Sounds ridiculous, doesn't it? I mean, you know I don't like being in crowds of people I don't know. But this is kind of worse. This is a room full of people who all know real estate investing." Sawyer hands the plates to Hellen and bites on his bottom lip, displaying only his two front teeth, like a sarcastic bucktooth bunny rabbit about to get defensive on something he knows nothing about. "And they know how to talk the BIZ. They know the 'lingo.' Seriously, what kind of nerds go to these things?"

Hellen snorts, then composes herself, as if she were the coach of a college championship softball team. "You know you always go into mocking and name-calling mode as a form of defense. You do it to convince yourself you don't want to go, but really, how do you know everyone at that meeting is an expert? How do you know? And how do you know they all want to talk to Mr. big bad amazing Sawyer Abernathy?"

With a slight roll of her eyes, she scoops up a slice and puts it on his plate, waving the spatula around as if it were a laser pointer. "What you need to do is quit telling yourself these stories. These stories that you build up in your head and that never come true. Tell me this, Mr. Abernathy. When's the last time one of the stories you've built up in your head and told yourself repeatedly actually became true?" Hellen turns back to scooping slices and filling plates. "What you need to do is go to that meeting. Stop thinking about it. Don't think about it again; just go. I'll go with you. Do you want me to?"

"No, no, you're right. I do need to quit thinking and just go. And I need to go alone; just something I need to do."

"Great. That's settled. These smell amazing. Pizza's ready! Let's eat!"

***

YOUR NEXT STEPS TO MAKE AN OFFER:

- ☐ Introspection Exercise: Self-reflecting is a healthy exercise to collaborate your internal barometer, your internal compass. There are plenty of resources available on the internet, but for this book, I want you to focus on and really pay attention to how your body, your mood, and your attitude transition on the night before you must go to work. In Sawyer's case, this is Sunday night, and even Hellen recognized and could see a physical change in his appearance. If you're married or have close roommates, ask them if they notice your physical appearance or attitude changing on Sunday night.

    - *BONUS TIP*: If this person lives with you, ask them to verbally point out, albeit in a nice way since you're teetering on the edge of a depressing moment when they notice this change. Also, be receptive to this feedback. They are trying to help you.
    - *BONUS TIP #2*: Come up with a comical safe word or phrase that your "monitor" can use to comically let you know what they are seeing. This makes the interaction more well-received.

- ☐ Attend a Local REIA Meeting: At the end of Chapter 1, you applied some Google magic and found at least one local real estate investors association (REIA) or real estate investor meetup near you. Put the next meeting on your calendar and attend it (most of the time the first meeting is *free* to attend).

- *BONUS TIP*: Take a friend with you to this REIA meeting.
- *BONUS TIP* #2: If offered, sign up on every wholesaler's list at the meeting. This will help you with your deal flow, understanding what value add opportunities are out there, and increasing your overall knowledge.
- *BONUS TIP #3:* If attending in person is not your thing, register for and attend the *free Ask Me Anything* sessions at **www.W2Capitalist.com/MakeAnOffer**

- ☐ Who Do You Know: Talk to five more people about your ambitions to explore real estate investing. Again, ask them who they know that already invests and ask for that introduction. By the way, if these are in-person meetings, you're still buying that round of coffee, beers, or food.
- ☐ Proceed to Chapter 3.

CHAPTER 3

ATTICUS

"Now, one thing I tell everyone is learn about real estate. Repeat after me: real estate provides the highest returns, the greatest values and the least risk."

—Armstrong Williams

CHAPTER 3

Today started out like most any other day for Sawyer. He woke around 7:45, drug his butt slowly out of bed, went downstairs to their small white cabinet, granite countertop, L-shaped kitchen, poured himself a glass of lukewarm water straight from the faucet, inhaled the water with a few big gulps, and started back upstairs to his home office. *No admin today; just client visits. I've got to get on the road*, he thinks. "But wait!" Adrenaline flushes into his bloodstream like a jolt of lightning, rendering him immovable. "Shit! Tonight is the REIA meeting!" Struck with fear that he actually might go, Sawyer brushes off the fear as quickly as it came. "I have client visits today, so no way I'll be back for the meeting."

"Hun, are you OK? Who are you talking to?" Hellen asks.

With heart still racing, Sawyer awkwardly responds, "What? Oh, nothing, babe. Just realized how I need to get on the road, and I won't make it to the REIA meeting tonight. Have you seen my phone?"

Scrolling through available podcasts and loading up his phone with new material for today's road trip, Sawyer realizes months have gone by since he discovered the two local Real Estate Investing Association meetups, but he had yet to attend a meeting. Regardless of what excuse he kept telling himself to weasel out of not going, it comes down to one thing: his introverted personality.

This first one is free. Come on, Sawyer, live a little. Go network with other wannabe millionaires. Sawyer mocks his own inability.

He just couldn't bring himself to attend a meeting. Every time he thought about attending, those nightmare boyish feelings took him back to the middle school Sadie Hawkins dance where he had hidden in the corner all night, hoping and even praying that not a single girl would ask him to dance. And since Sawyer did not have any friends who were interested in investing, he didn't have the extra nudge that he was used to leaning on for social situations. Looking through his podcasts, he saw the title "How to Create the Perfect Partnership." Yes, maybe he needed a partner.

Sawyer's internal thoughts begin to fade away as he grabs his things and heads out the door for a day of customer visits—welp, let's call them what they are: complaint sessions, bitch sessions, just smile and nod sessions, "Thank you ma'am/sir. May I have another?" sessions.

Since the acquisition, Sawyer's customer meetings had become mundane. They were so repetitive that they were mind numbing. The kind of mind-numbing feeling you experience as you mow the lawn for what feels like the 151st time. No real conscious thought, an absolutely clear mind, just going through what has become commonplace.

After his last client for the day, Sawyer, feeling defeated, plops into his smoldering leather car seat, turns on the ignition, and hears his Bluetooth connect and pump out the remainder of the podcast he started this morning. His thoughts shift to the REIA meeting.

Wait, how am I supposed to find a partner if I can't muster up the courage to talk to anyone?

"Screw it. I'm going to the meetup tonight."

"Hellen," Sawyer says as she picks up the phone. "I'm going to do it. I'm going to the Real Estate Investing Association meetup tonight. I'm leaving my last customer now, and if traffic isn't horrible, I can make the meeting. I have no idea how long these things last, but I just need to do it."

"You go, babe! Do you want me to go with you?"

"No. This is something I want to do. This is something I need to do."

Sawyer is always amazed that no matter how much or how little he confided in Hellen, she always leaves him feeling confident, comfortable, and strong.

***

The clock rolls over to 10:07 p.m. This is the latest Sawyer has arrived home since they were married.

"Hey, babe, how did it go?" Hellen whispers as Sawyer sits on the bed next to her.

"Oh, it was great honey. Completely fantastic. It wasn't awkward at all. I met a few folks, including a guy named Atticus. He reminds me of Nic Nolte."

Hellen squints a smile as she snuggled back in. "That's great, honey. So, you're glad you went?"

"Yes. I mean what was I so scared of? And this guy Atticus is great. He and I are going to meet for coffee in the morning."

"Oh, wow. Great. I'm glad you went, and tomorrow sounds exciting. I'd love to talk more, but I'm super tired. Come snuggle me."

***

The following morning came quickly. By 6:45, Sawyer is showered, shaved, and bouncing out the door to go meet Atticus at the Brew & Hop.

"So here's the thing, Sawyer, investing criteria are investing criteria," stats Atticus.

What does that even mean—investing criteria are investing criteria, thought Sawyer as he just nods and smiles as if he understands everything Atticus is conveying.

"There's the fifty percent rule, the one percent rule, the two percent rule, cash-on-cash return, and the one everyone talks about is cash flow. What's your investing criteria, Sawyer?" Atticus sips his coffee.

"Well . . . Atticus, all of those sound really intriguing, but I have absolutely no idea what you're talking about. The one percent cash flow on equity and what was the other one? Internal equity on return of two percent?"

"No, no, no, no, no, no, you got it all wrong," Atticus announces in a hurriedly, raspy tone while taking another sip of his coffee and waving his hand in the air.

"Look, son, in order to invest, and invest without losing

any money, you need to not only learn all of the different and available investing criteria, but you need to establish your own.

"Now, Sawyer, why are you wanting to invest in real estate?"

Sawyer sits back in his rickety chair, ponders for a brief moment, and opens up.

"Atticus, I hate my job. I want to invest in real estate so that I don't have to work as much. I have a kid on the way, the company that I was a principal at sold out, I'm on my third boss since the acquisition happened just a few months ago, customers are leaving, I think I'm going to get fired . . ."

"Whoa, horsey, let's slow down just a bit," Atticus interrupts as gently as he can while taking another sip of joe. "So, ultimately, you want to invest for cash flow so that you can quit your job. Is that right?" asks Atticus.

"Yes."

"Ok, then. I'll give you a quick run-down of the rules and criteria for buying and holding rental properties. First things first, these rules are just rules of thumb. Think of them as napkin tests. They are a quick way to evaluate if you want to dive deeper into seeing if this potential property is something you want to explore or quickly decline. Once a potential property passes your napkin tests, then you'll want to dive into the actual calculations. And don't worry, there are some extremely cool, easy-to-use online calculators that make this easy. Trust me, Sawyer, if an old guy like me can use them, so can you."

- 50 percent rule: The fifty-percent rule is a simple way to see if the rent being charged will cover all the property's expenses. Typically, a rental property is effectively run if 50 percent of the rent being charged can cover all the expenses, except for the mortgage. So, in other words, plan on 50 percent of the rent going directly toward expenses. The remaining 50 percent will go toward the mortgage payment and to you in the form of profit (or cash flow).
- 1 percent rule / 2 percent rule: The 1 percent rule basically states the gross monthly rental income of a property is equal to 1 percent of the purchase price. An investment property with a $100,000 purchase price would need to rent for $1,000 a month to hit the 1 percent rule. The reason the napkin test is important is if you're potential property hits the 1 percent rule, you have a good idea of where the cash flow will land. If a $100,000 purchased property rents for $2,000 month in gross rental income, then that's the 2 percent rule. Properties that hit the 2 percent rule are generally in worse neighborhoods.
- Cash-on-cash return: From an equation standpoint, cash-on-cash return is calculated by dividing the annual pre-tax cash flow by the amount invested. Let's take your $100,000 purchased property. After all expenses are paid, the anticipated total amount of cash in your pocket after owning the property for 365 days is $1,800 ($150/month for twelve months). You purchased this

$100,000 property by putting 20 percent down or $20,000. 1,800 divided by 20,000 equals a 9 percent cash-on-cash return. This is a good metric to compare rental properties with other rental properties to see which one will give you the best-anticipated return.

- Cash flow: You must be careful with this one as many people calculate cash flow differently. Cash Flow is not gross rental income; cash flow is income minus expenses, and the expenses that should be included when calculating cash flow are: taxes, repairs, insurance, mortgage, management, and vacancy. To help you remember these, use the acronym TRIMMVC.

As Atticus continues to explain the finer details of these rules and criteria, Sawyer realizes how uplifting it felt to verbalize what weighed on him so heavily. Even though he had expressed these very same things to Hellen, who fully supported his ambitions, this feels different. It is as if Atticus knew exactly what he meant and how he feels.

Talking with Atticus, an almost stranger, with his experience and empathetic tones, is a completely different feeling. An uplifting, energizing tone. *How many more Atticuses were out there? Is it possible there are more that think this same way?*

"Sawyer? Hey, Sawyer." Atticus nudges Sawyer on the arm. "Hey, pal, you still with me? I feel like you zoned out for a minute."

"Yes, I'm here. Sorry about that. This is all a bit overwhelming. You've provided a lot for me to think about, and the one thing that I keep thinking is, How do I purchase an investment property. I mean, I don't have tons of cash just sitting in the bank collecting dust."

"Oh hell, Sawyer. You don't need a ton of money, and it's possible you have money in places you don't even realize."

"Oh yea, where? In my couch cushions?"

"Welp, not really, but maybe in the house where the couch sits."

Sawyer perks up. "Ok, what do you mean?"

"Well, if you've owned your house for any number of years, it's possible you have equity pinned up in it. Equity is just cash that isn't liquid. You tap into that equity through what's called a HELOC, a home equity line of credit. This is essentially a line of credit, like a credit card, with your house acting as collateral. Talk to your bank about potentially acquiring a HELOC. Now, it'll cost you a few hundred dollars for the appraisal, but most of the time, they waive the closing costs as long as you keep the HELOC open for X number of years. How long have you lived in your current place?"

"Not long, but we've had some houses in our neighborhood recently sell for *way* more than what we paid for ours."

"Alright, sounds like you may be onto something."

"Atticus, I can't thank you enough for this."

"Happy to help a newb anyway I can."

***

CHAPTER 3

"Hellen! Hellen," Sawyer yells as he bursts through the front door. "Investing criteria. We need to establish our investing criteria. Hellen? Hellen!"

"Yes, babe?"

"We need to establish our investing criteria! And we need to apply for a HELOC," announces Sawyer.

"I'm upstairs!"

As Sawyer makes his way upstairs, in his excitement, he takes the stairs two at a time, only tripping once. "We need to establish our investing criteria and apply for a HELOC."

As quickly as he could get the words out again about how they needed to establish their investing criteria, he realizes it is time for work. Admin day. "Hun, I have to log in for work, but this is it. This is what we need to do. Investing cri-ter-ria!!!"

***

After a full day of fun-loving work (note the sarcasm), Sawyer's momentum to talk about and research real estate investing criteria is depleted. He moseys downstairs, plops down on the loveseat, lies back, and covers his eyes with his forearm.

After a few mere moments, he feels the cold sweat of an ice-cold beer graze his open hand. "What's *our* investing criteria?" Hellen asks.

It takes several long nights and half the weekend of researching written articles and listening to numerous podcasts, but Sawyer, alongside Hellen, establishes their investing criteria:

- Minimum cash-on-cash return: 12 percent
- Minimum monthly cash flow: $150
- Zip Codes: 32501, 32503, 32563, 32571, 32570, 32565
- Single-family and small multifamily units (<=4 units) built after 1950
- Low-crime neighborhoods / no registered sex offenders in the community
- No flood zones

Reflecting at the computer screen, Sawyer says, "By George, I think we've got it! This theory holds water. That ship will sail!"

***

YOUR NEXT STEPS TO MAKE AN OFFER:

- ☐ Know Your Why: Before you start creating your investing criteria, you need to figure out *why* you want to become a real estate investor. The ultimate answer is not money. Almost everyone starts there, but you need to have a bigger purpose. Ask yourself *why* until you have this aha moment. This can be seven iterations, or this can be, like for me, more than fifteen. Knowing your why will help you establish your investing criteria and strategy. For example:

    - Q: Why do you want to invest in real estate?
    - A: I want to make more money.
    - Q: Why do you want to earn more money?
    - A: If I have more money coming in, then I don't have to stress so much about work.
    - Q: Why do you want to stress less about work?
    - A: Because it's not good for my health, and I want to be around and have the ability long term to enjoy life with my family.
    - Q: Why do you want to enjoy life with your family long term?
    - A: I don't get to spend enough time with them now because I'm living the rat race life.

- ☐ Create Your Investment Criteria: Everyone invests for different reasons, and as your investment career and experience evolve, your investing criteria will too, but we need to establish a starting point. Some guidelines, built-in railings, will help you find the properties worth seeking to help you accomplish your why. What deals or opportunities are you looking to grab and which ones should you stay away from? Having an established investing criteria will guide you through these uncharted waters. The more detailed your investing criteria, the more successful you'll be. Aim small, miss small.

- ☐ Tools for Calculating Returns: To see a more in-depth example of how I calculate cash flow and cash-on-cash return and use TRIMMVC, head to **www.W2Capitalist.com/MakeAnOffer.**
- ☐ Talk to One Lender: This is a phone call to your local/regional bank. This is a lending institution with one–five locations; it can be a credit union. Talk to them about your ambitions to start investing in real estate and ask what programs they offer. Now, I loathe banks and the financing process with traditional banks, and eventually, you will not need them, but for now, they are a necessary evil that have to be dated. Word of warning, they may ask you questions you don't know the answer to and that's the point of the exercise. Go find those answers.

  - *BONUS TIP*: Discuss Pulling a HELOC. If you currently own a home, talk to your bank about pulling a HELOC. The idea here is to get familiar with the process and even go through with it. Most HELOCs don't charge you anything to have it open and available, and it's always best to have the money ready and available and then find a deal, versus finding a deal and scrambling to find the money.

- [ ] Procced to Chapter 4.

CHAPTER 4

MENTAL ROADBLOCK

"if you're not going to put money in real estate, where else?"

—Tamir Sapir

CHAPTER 4

With the AC on full blast, the smell of worn-out deodorant and light sweat was hardly noticeable. Sawyer sits, in the leather seat with the sun visor flipped down, stuck in traffic on his way home from a day of client visits. Instead of focusing on the client complaints, the next dreaded call with his boss, and all the upcoming meetings that could have just been emails, Sawyer is laser-focused on his newfound love: real estate investing.

Since Sawyer and Hellen spent most of the weekend establishing their investing criteria, Sawyer has spent almost every wakening moment since thinking about how he could foster their investing career to begin. He was clear. He could see the vision, but with each new horizon, a new peak of questions and self-doubt would arise.

With $150 in monthly cash flow, it will only take sixty-seven doors to completely replace my salary. Wait a minute, sixty-seven doors? How the hell are we going to purchase sixty-seven doors? If we purchased five properties a year, that will take way too long. Maybe we can purchase ten. Yea, ten doors a year, and I'll be out of this place in five; fifteen doors a year, and I'll be out in four. Ahhh, I just need to get the first one done and then figure out how to scale.

"How do I make this first one happen!?!" Sawyer screams, breaking his own silence.

This is going to happen. Before I know it, I'll be out of this hellhole of a job.

With this clarity also came nervousness and anxiety. While Sawyer's plan made sense, he had no sense of confidence. None of his friends or family is doing this.

What if we lost money, what if we went bankrupt, what if . . .

"I can't afford anything extremely nice, so am I going to be a slum lord? Do I want to be a slum lord? Do I want to deal with that kind of tenant? Can I deal with that kind of tenant?" Sawyer questions aloud as the break of silence seemed to calm his nerves.

Feeling more anxious than normal, he decides to call Hellen.

"Hey, babe. What are you doing?"

"Getting dinner ready. When do you think you'll be home?"

"Probably around six; just got on the interstate. Hey, I've been thinking a lot today about us becoming real estate—"

"Me too!"

"Can we do this? I mean, do you think we can actually buy a property, find a tenant, manage it ourselves, and, most importantly, produce money doing it?"

"Yes, I do . . . but why do you ask that, in that way? Where's the doubt coming from?"

"I don't know. I mean I can see this so clearly. It's almost like reality is standing right slap in front of me. I feel it, staring me right in the face, and all I hear in my head are these doubtful voices: 'You can't do this, Sawyer! Who are you to be a real estate investor'? I mean, we're barely getting by now, so how we are going to afford a property that someone, some decent person, will actually rent?"

"I don't know, hun, but we'll figure it out. We can totally do this. Who's that guy you recently had coffee with? Atticus? Maybe he can give you some advice."

"Atticus. Yea. I'll call Atticus. Let me do that now on my way home. Thank you, my love! I'll see you soon."

***

"Atticus, it's Sawyer. We met last week for coffee," says Sawyer.

"Yea, hey Sawyer. How are ya, bud?"

"Great man. Hey, I wanted to thank you again for our conversation last week. Hellen and I spent the better part of last weekend working on our investing criteria. We have it nailed down, and things seem so much clearer now we believe we can do this, but now, well . . ."

"What is it, Sawyer? Spit it out, son."

"Well, I don't know what to do next. I felt like we had all this momentum as we worked through establishing our investing criteria, and today, I'm back at work, and—"

"And what? You're now back at work, and you're now having doubts that you can even do this? I'm not shocked, Sawyer. Who else have you talked to about investing beside me and Hellen? No one I bet."

Caught by surprise, Sawyer stammers, "Uhhh, yes, you're correct. Well, I'll have conversations here and there with guys I'm close to at work and socially I've known these guys for five–six years."

"Yea, and what do they tell you? That you're crazy? That real estate investing is a rich man's game, and it ain't for you? Look, Sawyer, you need to stop talking about real estate with those friends. They'll do nothing for you but hold you down. Come back to the REIA meeting next month. I'll be there. I'll introduce you to some other folks. You need new friends, Sawyer, plain and simple. I'll see you then."

Baffled at how accurate Atticus could be, Sawyer couldn't get past, nor believe that he needed new friends.

***

Exhausted from today's mileage, Sawyer plops into bed, laptop in hand.

"Hun, as always supper was amazing. Thank you."

"Thank you . . . and you're welcome. What's up with the laptop? More work tonight?"

"Not really. It was something Atticus encouraged."

"Oh yea, what did he say?"

"He stated we need new friends."

"New friends? Why do we need new friends?"

"Yea, new friends. Friends that are focused on real estate investing. I know your friends; you know my friends. I can't think of a single person who I can approach about this. Can you?"

CHAPTER 4

"You're right. I don't. So, what's the plan with your laptop?" She points to the laptop. "Is there a dating site for wannabe real estate investors?"

"Hashtag L-O-L" Sawyer cackled as he forms a hashtag with his fingers. "I don't think there is a J-Date for real estate investors, but there has to be something, right?"

"How about a mastermind?"

Sawyer looks at her in shock.

"What? I did some research today while you were gone. I was thinking about how stressed you were going to that REIA meeting, being in a crowd, feeling like a spotlight was on you. A smaller group is your style. Now to just find the right one.

"Mastermind structures appear to be all over the place. Free ones, ones that cost, some that are super expensive, some are in person, some are virtual. It appears you can really find one that just works for you."

As Hellen drifted off to incubation sleep, Sawyer is hard at work being a keyboard junkie looking for a mastermind. Distracted by the occasional, yet particularly loud, snoring coming from his partner's side of the bed, Sawyer shakes his head and diligently browses the internet for the right group, the right mastermind, the right community, the right tribe for him to join. Ideally, he wanted to join one where he could be himself and just observe until he grew comfortable talking and engaging with others, one where he wouldn't feel intimated when he wanted to ask a question. A mastermind that pushes him outside of his comfort zone but did so without costing a whole lot of money. In essence, just like Hellen and Sawyer created their investing criteria, Sawyer slowly starts creating his ideal mastermind criteria. Feeling accomplished and glancing at the bedside table clock flashing 3:30 a.m., Sawyer tiredly rubs his eyes, closes his laptop, puts it down on the bedside table next to him, and snuggles up to Hellen, who briefly awakes to embrace his hug.

"Morning Sunshine," Hellen says as she rolls over to nudge Sawyer to tell him his alarm is beeping. "How late did you stay up?"

"Pretty late, but I couldn't turn my brain off. The mastermind approach is a really good idea, Hellen, and I think I figured something out."

"Oh yea? What's that? How to love me even more?"

"No, no silly. I don't think that's even possible, but that is an interesting thought. I think I've figured out what I want from a mastermind."

"Cool, OK, let me hear it."

"Well, I like the idea of it being all virtual. You know when I get into crowds, I just don't do well—"

"Really?" Hellen says sarcastically. "You mean that scene at the Kenny Chesney beach concert wasn't abnormal?" Hellen and Sawyer both laugh as they give each other a light morning smooch and start to roll out of bed.

"Ha. No listen. A virtual mastermind means I can participate from anywhere. No leaving you in pregnant status while I'm out rubbing elbows in the evening. You know I don't like to be gone during the day for work already. Plus, it'll be less stress and anxiety for me. I'll be anxious enough being the newbie with all the stupid questions—"

"There is no such thing as a stupid question, Sawyer, but I like it. Please continue."

"Yea, so completely virtual, low budget. You know how we are tight on funds right now and man, these masterminds can get expensive. I watched some videos on these couple of guys last night. Man, I don't know how folks can't see right through them. They were charging $25,000 a year to join. I'm thinking like free!"

"Well, you know what they say. You pay for what you get."

"Yea, I know. And if we're going to take this seriously, I need to invest a little in it. We'll need to figure out what we can spend or what we can stop spending on so that I can join one. Maybe you can join one too?"

"Maybe, but I think I'm going to be pretty consumed over the next couple of months," Hellen states as she motions to her bulging, very pregnant belly.

***

YOUR NEXT STEPS TO MAKE AN OFFER:

- ☐ Calculate Your Financial Freedom Number: Because I know you are an amazing action taker, I know you've already created your investing criteria, but if you haven't, go back and do that now. Even if breaking free from the rat race isn't on your radar right now, go through this exercise of calculating your financial freedom number. It will serve as a barometric guide later. In our story, Sawyer calculates his number to only include his salary, but when you calculate yours, assuming your lifestyle choices are going to stay the same, use what's called a labor loaded rate. A good rule of thumb here is 20 percent on top of your annual salary to cover benefits like health, dental, and vision insurance, retirement planning, etc. So, if you make $100,000 a year, your financial freedom number (with the labor loaded rate of 20 percent) is $120,000. Of course, I'm making some assumptions. For example, you're living within your means of your current salary and able to save while investing or you are willing to make lifestyle changes to cut out spending. For more resources on calculating your financial freedom number, you guessed it, visit this book's resource page at **www.W2capitalist.com/MakeAnOffer**
- ☐ Join Your Local REIA and Attend Six Consecutive Meetings: This is the week you not only join your local REIA group, but you also commit to attending

every meeting for the next six months. Time block this on your calendar and go to every meeting.

- ☐ Proceed to Chapter 5.

CHAPTER 5

THUMP, THUMP, THUMP

"It is a comfortable feeling to know that you stand on your own ground. Land is about the only thing that can't fly away."

—Anthony Trollope

CHAPTER 5

Today's doctor visit with Hellen is loaded with anticipation and excitement. Of course, Sawyer is distracted, thumbing through all the work emails that were populating into his phone. "I thought you were off today," whispers Hellen as she leans into hug Sawyer.

"I am. I know, I know. Just if something comes up and I don't respond right away . . . I mean look at this!"

"Shhhhhh," playfully Hellen nudged. "Not so loud, we *are* at the doctor's office. Are you excited about the ultrasound? It's possible we'll get to hear the baby's heartbeat today."

"Yea, I am. This is all crazy, isn't it? We're about to see our baby for the first time. We need to remind the nurse that we don't want to know the sex of the baby, right? I mean, that is still something that you want to do, have the sex of the baby be a surprise?" Sawyer asks.

"Yes. I have told you a thousand times. Yes. It'll be the best surprise we will ever experience in our lives. Trust me on this one. And we don't have to tell the nurse today that we don't want to know the sex of the baby. We won't be able to tell for several more weeks, silly."

"Hellen? Hellen Abernathy?" the nurse calls into the waiting room.

"Come on. Let's go." Hellen nudges Sawyer as she gathers their things and begins to scamper toward the door the nurse is propping open. Sawyer quickly followed.

"Take a seat just to your right, ma'am. I need to check your vitals," the nurse urges Hellen as she shuffled by. As Sawyer approached the nurse who was holding the door waiting on him, he says, "Did she tell you? We don't want to know the sex of the baby. It's going to be a surprise."

"No she did not, but I'm just checking her vitals. She will need to be sure to tell the ultrasound tech when you get back there, but it might be a little early."

With vitals checked, it was Hellen's turn on the ultrasound table. As they entered the dimly lit, cooler room, Sawyer hollers, "Yea we don't want to know the sex!" interrupting Rachel, the ultrasound tech, who was giving Hellen some last-minute instructions and expectations on her first ultrasound.

"Ok, it might still be too early to tell, but I'll note that on your chart."

As Hellen hops on the ultrasound table and exposes her belly, she calmly reaches out to clutch Sawyer's hand. "You'll have to forgive my husband, Rachel. He is more nervous than I am."

With a squeeze of a bottle, Rachel empties the propylenic gel onto Hellen's belly. The sound makes Sawyer giggle. As Rachel begins to move the wand around Hellen's belly, Sawyer stops thinking about working and stressing over unread emails. He was in the moment. He was in that moment, and at the moment, he stared, blank-minded, into the monitor hanging above them. Attempting to decipher what was happening and not knowing what he was seeing, Sawyer feels Hellen squeeze his hand ever so gently as if to draw his attention to something fantastic that was about to happen. Rachel breaks the silence. "There it is. You see that little bean right there?" she says as she moves her mouse pointer near a blob on the screen. "That's your baby."

Hellen starts sniffling and begins to tear up. Sawyer, with a deeper blank stare and even more distant focus, slowly turns to Hellen with his mouth wide open. It was indescribably beautiful and suddenly became even more real. "I'm. Going. To. Be. A. DAD!" Sawyer screams to himself as he gently squeezes Hellen's hand.

"Do you want to hear the heartbeat?" asks Rachel.

The question did not need to be asked. Without a spoken word, they both nodded.

"Thump thump"

Sawyer's eyes instantly filled with water. He squeezes Hellen's hand even tighter. "*What is this emotion I feel right now*," he thinks as stares at the screen and tunes in once again for a listen.

"Thump thump"

"One hundred fifty beats per minute. That's a healthy baby," says Rachel, but Sawyer barely hears her. He doesn't even notice the ultrasound is over, that Rachel is cleaning up Hellen and helping her off the table.

"I'm going to be a dad," Sawyer says under his breath as he sits back.

"Sawyer? Are you OK, hun?" Hellen asks. Afraid to speak, fearing that if he did, he would start uncontrollably sobbing, he mumbles. "Yes." Hellen motions him to get up. "Great. Now c'mon. We have to go see the doctor now."

With Hellen's doctor visit complete, Sawyer and Hellen head to Applebee's, a new tradition they established. Hellen would always get the oriental chicken salad; Sawyer would alternate between the Fiesta Lime Chicken or a hamburger. Even though hearing that little bean's heartbeat was cause for a Fiesta, today was a hamburger day: medium, all the fixings, side of French fries, honey mustard. "Applebee's has the best honey mustard," Sawyer says.

Sawyer is nervously chatting about anything that could take his mind off the fear that bubbles inside of him when he thinks about becoming a dad.

CHAPTER 5

"Thump thump thump thump thump thump thump thump," echoes in Sawyer's head as Hellen breaks the silence.

"Babe? What are you in deep thought about?"

"Huh? Who me?" stutters Sawyer, unsuccessful at playing it cool. "Oh nothing." To divert the ensuing conversation, and his thoughts, away from that amazing, but believable, tears of joy and fear-producing ultrasound heartbeat, Sawyer blurts out the first thing that came to his mind: "Driving for dollars."

"Driving for dollars? What's that?"

"Well, babe," Sawyer begins with an inkling of confidence, "we essentially drive neighborhoods where we want to invest, and if we see a house—"

"OK, so who gets the oriental chicken salad?" the waitress interrupts.

"I do," says Hellen.

"Here ya go," says the waitress, "and then this one must be yours. Y'all enjoy."

As they both snag their utensils, Sawyer continues, "That was weird. How could she not remember what each one of us just ordered? Never mind; it doesn't matter. Yea, driving for dollars. We drive neighborhoods or areas that we want to invest in and we look for properties that have overgrown yards, have boarded-up windows, or appear abandoned. We then write the addresses down, find the owner's contact information, send them a letter, and give them a call to let them know we want to buy their property. We buy it and manufacture the cash flow. Bada bing, bada boom. Plus, we get to deduct the mileage we used as a business expense on our taxes." Sawyer begins to wave his knife and fork at Hellen as if he's conducting an orchestra. "Ya know. Driving. For. Dollars."

Hellen raises her baton, a salad fork, and motions a three-beat to Sawyer. "Driving. For. Dollars." And with another round of conducting an orchestra, she says, "Sounds. Like. A. Plan."

As she finishes her bite, she asks, "Where do we begin?"

"We begin right after we finish here. We'll take the long way home. I have a few neighborhoods I've been thinking about, streets I've never driven on. I'd like to start there. Sound good to you?"

Hellen agrees. "Sounds good to me."

"Great," Sawyer says. "Now how about that ultrasound? I mean we just heard the heartbeat of our *kid*!"

***

CHAPTER 5

YOUR NEXT STEPS TO MAKE AN OFFER:

- ☐ Drive for Dollars: It doesn't matter if you're doing a coffee run, driving to the office, running to the grocery store, or heading to a doctor's appointment. Wherever you are going, start driving different routes than you normally take. This will give you a perspective you've never seen before on the neighborhoods around you. Start sharpening your eye by finding homes where the grass is taller and stays taller than the rest of the homes around it. Look for properties that are in dire need of a fresh coat of paint and properties that you never see a car in the drive. Make special dates to drive for dollars in the zip codes you identified when you established your investing criteria. For technological help to keep all these properties organized, check out the tools I use when I Drive for Dollars at **www.W2capitalist.com/MakeAnOffer**
- ☐ Underwrite Ninety Properties in Thirty Days: Start with underwriting just one property today. Go find a property, listed on any of the popular listing sites, in the area you identified in your investing criteria created at the end of Chapter 3, and underwrite that property. There are going to be tons of questions that you don't know the answers to, and that's the purpose of this exercise. If you have never underwritten a property, it could take you up to two hours to complete this challenge today. Underwrite three properties a day so

you have ninety properties by the end of thirty days. By doing this, you will have exponentially grown your knowledge about the market you're targeting and verified and possibly made adjustments to your investing criteria. After doing this challenge, you'll be able to underwrite three properties in as little as fifteen minutes on the back of a napkin. To learn about the tools I use to make underwriting easier and more efficient, visit this book's resource page at **www.W2Capitalist.com/MakeAnOffer.**

- ☐ Acceptance: Regardless of what you have going on in life, whether it be a baby on the way, upcoming marriage or proposal, a new position at work, or taking care of a loved one, accept that becoming a real estate investor will take longer than you want it to. Progress over perfection is your focus here. Carve out thirty minutes to an hour every day to focus on REI, more if you're willing and able, but don't lose sight that this is a marathon and not a sprint. Once you close your first deal, the next one will come a lot easier. The deal after that will be even easier, and easier, and easier as you gain that momentum. Acceptance does not mean giving yourself an excuse to not put in the time and do the work. Time-blocking has been a major key to my success. More info on time-blocking can be found on this book's resource page at **www.W2Capitalist.com/MakeAnOffer**. And speaking of doing the work . . .
- ☐ Proceed to Chapter 6.

CHAPTER 6

EAST OR WEST

"Buy on the fringe and wait. Buy land near a growing city! Buy real estate when other people want to sell. Hold what you buy."

—John Jacob Astor

CHAPTER 6

Over the next couple of months after each of Hellen's doctor visits, they take the long way home to drive for dollars. After only a couple of visits, Sawyer compiled this process into a more efficient and effective strategy. The night before the planned doctor visits, they'd sit down on the couch, laptop in hand, with *The Office* playing in the background, and comb through the MLS, Craigslist, and Realtor sites, hunting for potential properties that hit their investing criteria, and chart a course for tomorrow's office visit while snickering at Kevin swimming in chili on the office floor.

"Hey, babe? What do you think about this one? This cute little yellow house?" Hellen whispers as she hands Sawyer her phone to show him the foreclosure listing she found.

"Hmm. You know what the 'experts' claim. To appeal to the masses, rental properties should be three bedrooms with two baths. This is a one-bedroom, one-bath." Sawyer stares intently at the screen. "But I can't get over that price. Something must be wrong with this place. It is on the east side of town, and you know we haven't seen anything in this price range on the east side. And it appears it has been on the market for a while, which is also odd. Either way, I'm intrigued. Let's drive by it tomorrow."

***

On the way back from Hellen's OB visit, they drove directly to the cute little yellow house's address. Driving for dollars again, but this time with a mission. As they pull onto East Main Street for the third time, lighthearted conversation about how cute the houses are fills the air (along with the smell of Applebee's leftovers and the anxious tension that was building. Each time they circled the block and did not find the little yellow house, their anxiety grew).

"Did we miss the address every time? Is this property going to be one of those where only the driveway is visible from the road?" Sawyer says in frustration as he pulls up to the curb, places the car in park, and picks up his phone, quickly tapping on the screen. "Oh, check this out. The address is actually 652 *West* Main Street, not east. Hmmm . . . I don't know how I feel about the west side," Sawyer says, already feeling defeated. "I knew this was too good to be true."

"We don't know that yet. I don't know anything about West Main Street either, but we won't know unless we go check it out," Hellen encourages. "After all, it is on our way home."

"Ok, let's go check it out. I mean it is only seven minutes away."

Moments later, Hellen points out the window. "There she is. The Little Yellow House."

"Oh, yes," says Sawyer. "There she is. I hardly noticed as my attention was drawn to that dump." Sawyer pointed out the windshield to the dilapidated, "hadn't seen a paint brush in thirty years, almost falling" shed that was directly across the

CHAPTER 6

street from the little yellow house. "I mean what is that? Do people actually live there?" Sawyer says in disbelief as he gazes at the handful of hoopties parked alongside the street and in the yard. "You can tell they park there a lot because there's almost no grass in the yard. Well, there is no grass; just patchy parts of weeds and sand."

"Yea, but we're not potentially buying that one; we're investigating in this one," says Hellen as she places her left hand underneath Sawyer's chin and turns his head toward the little yellow house. "I like it. We should set up a showing,"

"Oh, I don't know. You hear location, location, location, and I'm eyeballing what's across the street and I'm embarrassed I didn't bring my pistol with me today."

"Agreed, but peek down the street, on both sides." Hellen points at two different houses that are showing signs of being renovated. She turns to glance out the back window. "And look, there are two houses that way that are also being worked on. Maybe this is one of those areas that's going through a rejuvenation. I think we should inspect it. Let's call the Realtor."

Sawyer sits quietly for a moment, just staring out the driver's side window toward the little yellow house and away from Hellen. A cold sweat begins to brew as he visualized what reality would look like if they owned this property. He turns back toward Hellen. "I don't know. It—"

"Yes, my name is Hellen and my husband, and I would like to view the property at 652 West Main Street. Yes, the little yellow house."

After a little bit, she hangs up the phone.

"Ummm . . . who was that?" asks Sawyer.

"That was Wilmer. He's the Realtor on the property, and he'll be here in just a few minutes to open it up for us."

"Wait, what? We can just view a property like that?"

"Apparently, you can. I mean he is the Realtor, and he offered it. He said his office is right around the corner, and he'll be here in about five minutes."

The next five minutes seem like an eternity to Sawyer. No words are spoken. He just sits there, windows rolled up, doors locked and blankly stares out the driver's side window. Hellen is browsing for baby clothes and decoration tips on her phone.

A dark SUV with tinted windows pulls up in front of them. A short, stocky guy, with grey hair, hops out and drifts up to Sawyer's side and waves. Sawyer slowly rolls his window down.

"Hey, ya'll. I'm Wilmer. Let me go in and open her up. Give me just a few minutes and then y'all follow me," Wilmer says as he turns and starts meandering toward Little Yellow.

When they stepped in, they were hit with an oddly familiar smell of musk. "Yep, this one has been foreclosed for a while; I suggest you don't open the fridge. The power is not on, so it's a good thing ya'll called when you did so we could look at this while we still had some daylight. Are y'all wanting this for a rental?" questions Wilmer.

Hellen steps off to explore the one bedroom. Sawyer, acting like he knew what he is doing, opens the mechanical closet and stares at an HVAC system that appeared to come over on the Mayflower. "Yes, sir. We are wanting this as a rental. Know anything about the neighborhood?"

As Wilmer begins to answer, he is interrupted by Hellen yelling from the bedroom, "Sawyer, Come! Check this out!"

When he breaks the threshold of the bedroom door, he sees her. Hellen stands in front of the walk-in closet like a showcase model on the Price Is Right. "We don't even have closets this big!" Her eyes bulged with disbelief and hysterical chuckles, indicating she is in love.

"Yep, you could almost make this into a two-bedroom if you wanted," Wilmer chimes in.

"That is odd, right?" Sawyer asks.

"Well, you certainly don't see it much, especially in houses that were built in this era. This is a 1950s–'60s build. I have the paperwork in my truck. I'll go grab it and get you the exact date."

"Hellen, I know you're excited. But this is the kind of paneling we had in my college apartment. I mean this place was a shithole. What would we do with this?"

"You know the paneling is in pretty good shape. We could leave it as-is or put a coat of paint on it. You know this bedroom isn't very big—"

"Yea, the closet is almost as big as the bedroom. Are we sure we're not standing in the closet and that's the bedroom?" Sawyer jokingly asks as he points toward the closet.

With an appreciative grin for his attempt at humor, Hellen continues, "It's not that big of a bedroom. But we can lighten it up with a coat of paint. With a lighter colored paint, this room will seem bigger, and it will produce a nicer feel."

"Ok, what about the carpet?" Sawyer asks.

"Yea, that carpet has got to go."

"How much do you think it'll cost to replace the carpet?"

Wilmer came back at that moment. "For a space this small, a few hundred bucks. If you guys are planning on using this as a rental, you don't want to buy the expensive stuff. You're going to be replacing it every few years anyway."

"What's the non-expensive stuff? What kind of price are we talking about?" Sawyer asks Wilmer.

"Only a dollar, maybe two, per square foot if you have them put down a nice thick pad. Not expensive. For a room this size, three, maybe four hundred dollars . . ." Wilmer continues, but Sawyer is zoned out. His mind travels elsewhere to hoopties and drugs, anticipating murders and shots fired, the cost to paint the walls, carpet installation, and fix the archaic furnace . . ."

"Sawyer," Hellen says, bringing him back to the present moment. "Wilmer said this house was built in 1960. C'mon, let's go check out the kitchen and bathroom. "

"Ya'll do that. I'm going to step outside. I'll see you out there when you're finished," says Wilmer.

After they survey the rest of the house and step back onto the front porch Wilmer asks, "What do y'all think?"

Hellen gazes up at Sawyer. Sawyer says, "I don't know. I'm concerned about that over there. What can you tell me about this neighborhood and what's going on with that property?"

"The neighborhood is on the upswing. When y'all leave here, just drive around. You'll see new construction and a lot of rehabs in progress. As far as that over there"—he motioned toward the yard full of hoopties— "I can't say much about it. I know it doesn't appear good, but there doesn't seem to be any crime going on. At least not that I can research. This could potentially be your first rental property, correct?" Wilmer asks.

Sawyer stands blank-faced.

"Yes," Hellen says sharply.

"Great, then I think this could be a really good first rental for y'all. It's in a neighborhood that is on the upswing. You don't really have to do anything to the outside of it, and the inside just needs a little cleanup and paint. I mean being your first deal, I would recommend getting an inspection on it, but this is an as-is contract on this foreclosure. You won't have any negotiation power if the inspection turns up anything, but at least you'll know if it's worth moving forward on. And that price, I mean, what about that price?" Wilmer smiles. "If you are focused on cash flow, this is a good place to start. The purchase price is $25,000, and with some elbow grease and another $5,000, you'll have this place rent ready. Properties in this area will easily rent for $5, maybe $600 a month. After your expenses are paid, you're looking at $250 to $350 in monthly cash flow, easy. Plus, if you're nervous about the neighborhood, drive around. Lots of remodels happening two blocks that way and two blocks this way." Wilmer motions down the street.

Hellen and Sawyer glanced at one another. Their bodies tingled with emotion as if their gut feelings were somehow synchronously aligned and they knew exactly what they should do next. It was as if Wilmer was preaching directly to them and he already knew their criteria.

"Look, I can tell you two have a lot to think about. You have my number. I'm going to close the house up. You kids call me with any questions, but I suggest you not wait long if you're going to make an offer," Wilmer says as he shakes both their hands and exchanges goodbyes.

***

CHAPTER 6

YOUR NEXT STEPS TO MAKE AN OFFER:

- ☐ View a Property: Find a property that is on the market and that hits all of your investing criteria, call the listing agent, and schedule a showing. It's hard to believe at this point, but soon, you'll be so confident in your numbers, knowing your market and yourself, that you'll be able to make offers without ever stepping foot inside a potential property, but for now, build your confidence by finding and viewing a property that hits all your investing criteria. If you're super nervous about this one, bring a friend or mentally set your expectations that you're just going window shopping. You're not buying today; just browsing.
- ☐ Talk to One More Lender: This is a phone call to your local/regional bank. Like before, this is a lending institution with one–five locations; could be a credit union. Talk to them about your ambitions to start investing in real estate and ask what programs they offer. Word of warning, they may ask you questions you don't know the answer to, and that's the point of the exercise. Go find those answers.
- ☐ Proceed to Chapter 7.

CHAPTER 7

MAKE THE CALL

"Every person who invests in well-selected real estate in a growing section of a prosperous community adopts the surest and safest method of becoming independent, for real estate is the basis of wealth."

—Theodore Roosevelt

CHAPTER 7

Sawyer loved to fish.

On this day of fishing, Sawyer's day off, he went alone as Hellen wasn't feeling up to it. The pregnancy had her physically drained.

Sunburnt and with an empty cooler, Sawyer putters the boat back to the dock from a much-needed and relaxing day of unplugging and unwinding. Zero caught fish. It did not matter. Sawyer just loved being on the water. Days like today were what he lived for: no distractions, no thoughts of clients, no conversations from his boss taunting the mantra "Do less with more." It was a refueling to his soul.

When he is almost back to the dock, idle speed only, his phone rings. It is one of his biggest clients. Reluctantly, Sawyer answers. "Hey, Jerry, what's up?"

Jerry lit into him like a windmill in a tornado.

"Do you know what's going on with our servers? None of the doctors can get in!? Why aren't you fixing this?" On and on Jerry went, complaining and yelling at Sawyer.

"Jerry, JERRY! I'm sorry, Jerry. I'm not sure what's going on. I am off today, saw that it was you, and thought I'd answer. I don't have access to my computer now to investigate. I should be home in about thirty minutes. If you can wait—"

Jerry hangs up. Relieved that the phone call is over but very well knowing that he would have to deal with this later,

Sawyer feels outraged and angry at himself that he even answered the phone.

"It's my day off!"

In his anger, he doesn't notice how close he is to the dock, and he is coming in hot.

Luckily, no one else is around.

Anticipating the impending crash, with his heart jack-hammering, Sawyer mistakenly hammers down on the throttle and ramps up onto the dock!

"Holy shit!" Sawyer thunders as he gathers himself. His angry fog lifted, and the reality of what just happened became clear.

"I can't believe I blacked out for a moment." *What if Hellen would have been on here, and the baby? What could have happened to the baby??* "Something has to change."

***

Later that evening, Hellen and Sawyer are resting on the living room couch. Continuing their nightly routine. Sawyer blankly watches *The Office* reruns and tries not to think about the hellacious day he anticipates tomorrow. Hellen is browsing her phone for baby gift ideas. Both are waiting for supper to finish cooking, and Sawyer is subconsciously counting to prevent the need to hear the buzzing sound of the oven timer. Hellen sits up, places her phone on the coffee table, grabs the TV remote, and presses the mute button.

"So, what do you want to do, babe?" asks Hellen.

CHAPTER 7

"What do you mean?" He knows exactly what Hellen is referring to, but is hoping if he doesn't bring it up, and they don't talk about it, he won't be forced to deal with the stress and anxiety that goes along with it. He'd rather just sit there and soak up more of *The Office* theme song.

"Well, it's been a few days, and Wilmer said if we wanted to make an offer, we better do so quickly."

"Yea, but that's what every used-car salesman tells a potential client," says Sawyer. "I mean if it was such a hot commodity, why has it been sitting on the market for so long? And now suddenly we start hunting for our first deal, and we trigger the centrifugal forces that jinx this ugly duckling into everyone's sole desire?"

"I don't know, but at that price point, why wouldn't we do it? What is the worst-case scenario here?"

"The worst-case scenario is we buy a house in the hood, and one of us gets shot while working on the repairs or doing maintenance, and that little kangaroo"—Sawyer points to Hellen's belly and continues to rant—"grows up with just one parent."

"Sawyer, we both know that's not going to happen. Besides, you said it yourself, the neighborhood isn't that bad, and things are starting to turn around. What do you think we can get for rent there?"

"Well, Wilmer claims $5 to $600."

"Ok, so does that hit our investing criteria? Does that hit the one or two percent rule you were telling me about? You mentioned we should be focused on cash flow. How does this cash flow?" Hellen pauses and waits.

And waits . . .

And waits . . .

"Yes," mumbles Sawyer.

"Yes, what?" Hellen says.

"Yes, it creates cash flows. More cash flow, actually, than our minimum requirement. I mean Wilmer was right. I looked at other rentals in that area, and we could easily get high $500s or even $600 in rental income. And, yes, it hits our criteria of a low-crime neighborhood, even though the house across the street appears sketchy. And yes, yes, we're even above the one percent rule. The two percent rule even Hellen," Sawyer responds. "You do understand the 2 percent rule right, Hellen?" Sawyer turns to comical sarcasm that Hellen does not like. He continues, "Ya see, Hellen, if we're all in for $30,000 and our monthly rental income is $600, that there is the two percent rule! Does that make sense?"

The tension in the room was lifting and their conversational mood was lighting up.

With a slight roll of her eyes, she says, "Yes. Yes, I know the two percent rule Saw-YOUR. So, why wouldn't we do this?"

With a very focused and determined stare, Sawyer breaks his silence. "I don't know. I don't know why I can't get over this hurdle. It is nothing but a mental hurdle. We've done our homework. We know what we want. We know the market. We know the neighborhood. I just can't come to terms with making an offer because . . . because what if I do, and it gets accepted. . . . What then? And I don't know why I'm trying to overcomplicate this. This is what we want to do, this is where we want to go, this opportunity is what we've been searching for, for months. This is what's going to help us build a better future for us and that little bean in that kangaroo pouch of yours. I feel as if I stepped up to the major league plate of life, ready to take a swing, and then suddenly, I'm that five-year-old kid on the T-ball field who must glance back at his coach to get the nod of approval that its OK to chop some wood! What is wrong with me?"

"There's nothing wrong with you. We've never done this before. You've never done this before. And, yes, while we've done our homework, we don't know what might happen. And, yes, while it's an inexpensive first property, it is a lot of money to us. I think being scared, especially on your first deal, should be expected, especially when you don't have anyone around you that's doing this. But to me, that's what makes this whole scenario even better. We've done *our* homework. We've established *our* criteria. We've found *our* first deal. It seems like our next step is to submit an offer, and then we can worry about what to do if it gets accepted." Hellen sits back and waits.

And waits some more.

"Ok." Sawyer finally breaks the silence.

"Ok, what?"

"Ok, you're right. There really is nothing to fear. Let's call Wilmer and put in an offer." Sawyer feels relieved at the sound of those words.

***

YOUR NEXT STEPS TO MAKE AN OFFER:

- ☐ Writing Challenge: Today's challenge is to write down your biggest fears about pursuing real estate investing. Write down your biggest fear about closing on your first investment property. Once you have those written down, turn those fears into positive momentum. If you struggle with converting your fears to positive momentum, join me for a *Ask Me Anything* session. You can register for the next session by going to **www.W2Capitalist.com/MakeAnOffer**. If you don't want to reveal your fears in front of a bunch of strangers, choose one of the ten people you've been meeting with in person from Chapters 1 and 2. Which reminds me, we haven't done that in a while.
- ☐ Who Do You Know: Talk to five more people this week about your ambitions to explore real estate investing, but this time meet them somewhere in the market you want to invest in and take a different route to the meeting location than you normally would. Again, ask them who they know that already invests and ask for that introduction, then go over your fears list and brace for the impact of them saying, "You're not alone."
- ☐ Find and Connect with Three Realtors: Find and connect with three Realtors that serve the area you identified in your investing criteria. The best Realtor will prove to be an invaluable resource

during your investing journey, but you need to find them first. For a list of the questions you need to ask during your Realtor interviews, head over to **www.W2Capitalist.com/MakeAnOffer**.

- ☐ Proceed to Chapter 8.

CHAPTER 8

SKILLS ALIGNMENT

"You don't have to be great at something to start, but you do have to start to be great at something."

—Zig Ziglar

CHAPTER 8

The following morning, Sawyer's alarm goes off as he rolls out of bed. *Client meetings*, Sawyer thinks. After drinking a glass of water, taking a shower, and reviewing his audiobook for the upcoming drive, he kisses Hellen on the lips and heads out the door. Sawyer doesn't bring up their next step, calling Wilmer, to submit an offer on Little Yellow. Hoping that Hellen wouldn't either, he hurries out the door as quickly as he can. As he cranked his car and slowly pulled out of the drive, the audiobook begins to play:

"The reality is that we're lonely . . . we're supposed to be the lone wolf, the sole leader, the alpha, but deep down we want to be able to talk about our struggles. We want other men to bounce ideas off of. We want someone to help us be accountable. We want to join the battle for our lives with our brothers in arms. Unfortunately, we've bought into the idea that reaching for guidance, direction and brotherhood isn't manly at all. We started to believe the notion that the self-made man was the highest achievement any man could obtain . . . When we attempt to isolate ourselves and shield our experiences, thoughts, and emotions from others, we limit our growth and expansion. Our ancestors knew this. For as long as man had been on this planet, we have been forming packs and tribes. They knew that if they had any hope for survival they would need to come together as

an opportunity to accommodate each other's strengths and weaknesses." [1]

Sawyer leans in. "Wow was this book written for me?" he thinks to himself as he leans in to consume more.

"What Kipling means is that the pack, our friends, family, neighborhoods, and communities are only as strong as the individual members of that pack, us. And the individual members of that pack, are only as strong as the pack they live in. Thousands of years ago this was common knowledge, but today we are more disconnected than we have ever been . . . our need to congregate, to stay safe and secure, and to expand, have declined."

Sawyer pauses his new audiobook, to clear the air waves for the deep thought he was already into. "Packs, tribes . . . who is my pack, who is my tribe?" Sawyer asks. "If I examine who I'm around, who I spend the most of time with, other than the support of Hellen, my tribe, my pack is full of guys who, while are upset with their current job situation, are just searching for another job. They don't want to be independently wealthy. They don't even want to own rental properties or invest in real estate at all. I really need to change my tribe."

"You have a choice to make. Do you stick your head in the sand and pretend everything is normal, or do you step into the unknown? Face the reality of your own inadequacies and give your chance to be something more . . . it's easy to listen to a podcast on the way to a job that you don't enjoy. It's easy to read

---

1 *Michler, R. (2018). Sovereignty: The Battle for the Hearts and Minds of Men*

a few pages of a book and get all hyped up."

Pause. Sawyer sits in awe of the audio gospel of reality that just punched him in the face. Play.

Michler continues, "When I talk with my financial advisory clients, we don't talk about removing risk first. We talk about what risks they are willing to take relative to the return they hope to receive. The same idea is true as you embark on a journey that has the potential to change your life for the better . . . you might be living right now with the false idea that you are safe."

Pause. *Why the hell or what the shit am I so scared about when it comes to the little yellow house?* Sawyer thinks to himself as he pulls into a parking spot at his client's office. *Little Yellow hits all of our criteria, is projected to produce more cash flow than we anticipated, and we're using a HELOC. Oh, what if we don't get approved for the HELOC? I need to get over this mental hurdle, and I need to get over it now. What if someone else does snatch up this property now? What if we don't get approved for the HELOC? Then we would lose our earnest money deposit? Wait! What if we lose the property?!*

A vibrating sound from the cup holder where Sawyer's phone sits breaks his train of thought.

"Appointment reminder. Shit. Here we go," Sawyer says aloud to himself as he turns off his car, grabs his leather padfolio, puts on a smile, and marches into the first of today's challenging client meetings.

***

"Hey, Hun?" Hellen says when Sawyer got home. "I was listening to this book today."

"Oh, yea?" Sawyer perks up. "Well, what was it about? And when did you learn how to download audio books?" Sawyer's sense of humor was part of why Hellen was in love with him.

"It said, 'Hone the drills of your day job that are going to serve you in your dream job.' I mean, don't you negotiate deals at work?"

"Yes."

"Don't you manage your work schedule to an amazing degree of effective efficiency?"

"Yes."

"Aren't you having tough conversations with physician board members who are 'unhappy' with your company's service?"

"Yes, but why are you asking me—"

"And aren't you a certified project manager?"

"Yes, babe. What book are you reading?" Sawyer pleas jokingly.

"Well, the name of the book is *Quitter* by Jon Acuff, but here's my point: 'Hone the drills of your day job that are going to serve you in your dream job.' Sawyer, we both know that you're not in your dream job. I know that you're putting yourself under immense pressure, but let's face it, you already have the skills to be a real estate investor."

What other parallels to real estate investing do I already have that Hellen didn't mention, Sawyer briefly thinks to himself. Then, an epiphany strikes with a bolt of confidence that propels him into action. He immediately knows his next step.

Sawyer marches over to the kitchen, grabs his phone off the cool granite, unplugs the charger, and calls Wilmer.

"Wilmer, it's Sawyer. We want to submit an offer on West Main Street. What do you need from us?"

***

YOUR NEXT STEPS TO MAKE AN OFFER:

- ☐ Writing Challenge: Today's writing challenge is to write down your skills, whether they are personal or professional skills, and how those skills could benefit your REI ventures. If you struggle with paralleling skills you've already mastered into pursuing investing in real estate, join us for a free *Ask Me Anything* session that is designated just for folks like you. You can register for the next session by going to **www.W2Capitalist.com/MakeAnOffer**. If you don't want to reveal your skills in front of a bunch of strangers, then choose one of the many people you've been meeting in person from Chapters 1, 2, and 7.
- ☐ Find Your Tribe: Because you are an action taker, I know you've already joined your local REIA, but now let's focus on improving your inner circle. You need to find your tribe and join a mastermind. Watch the eleven-minute video titled *5 Things You Need to Consider Before Joining a Real Estate Investing Mastermind* on the resource page at **www.W2Capitalist.com/MakeAnOffer**. Spoiler alert, those five things are (1) does the size of the mastermind matter, (2) selection criteria, (3) cost/budget, (4) time commitment, and (5) what are your goals for joining. Of course, I want to invite you to apply to join the W2 Capitalist Mastermind. You can find more info at **www.W2Capitalist.com/Mastermind**, and when you're serious about joining, book a call with one of our

Membership Strategists at **www.W2Capitalist.com/BookACall.**

- ☐ Who Do you Know: You've seen this one three times already, and it keeps coming up because of how important this is. Talk to five more people this week about your ambitions to explore real estate investing, but this time meet them somewhere in the market you want to invest in and take a different route to the meeting location than you normally would. Again, ask them who they know that already invests and ask for that introduction, then go over your skills list and ask for help in identifying how those skills might benefit you in real estate investing.
- ☐ Talk to One More Lender: This is the final lender task in this book, but don't let your search for the perfect lending partner stop here. Again, this is a phone call to your local/regional bank. Like before, this is a lending institution with one–five locations; can be a credit union. Talk to them about your ambitions to start investing in real estate and ask what programs they offer. Reminder, they may ask you questions you don't know the answer to, and that's the point of the exercise. Be open, transparent, and go find those answers.
- ☐ Proceed to Chapter 9.

CHAPTER 9

ATTICUS, AGAIN

"The greatest glory in living lies not in never failing, but in rising every time we fall."

—Nelson Mandela

CHAPTER 9

"Alright, Sawyer, now that you're under contract, you'll want to get a home inspection done. You only have seven days for your inspection period, so be sure to get one lined up soon. You do have a home inspector, don't you?" asks Wilmer.

The answer is no. Sawyer doesn't have a home inspector. In fact, he isn't sure what a home inspector would provide him that he doesn't already know. The property is empty, the power is off, and they saw what it looked like. "Well, if you have one you prefer, I'll take the connection," Sawyer says.

"I'll text it to you. His name is Allan."

"Who was that?" Hellen politely asks as she waddles into the room.

"Huh? Oh, that was Wilmer. We are officially under contract!" Sawyer gushes as he dances over, gives her a hug and a peck on the cheek, and then puts his nose on her belly. "Did you hear that, little kangaroo bean? Mommy and Daddy are officially under contract on our first rental property."

Turning to Hellen, he says, "But Wilmer says we need to get a home inspection. I don't know why."

"Well, it doesn't have anything to do with how we purchase the property, but an inspection has everything to do about ensuring we know what we're buying, and we'll need a four-point and wind mitigation report so that we can take advantage of all credits that are available to us to reduce our insurance premium."

Sawyer stands in awe of the words coming out of her mouth. Had Hellen secretly snuck her pregnant body off to real estate investing school without him knowing it?

"Well, Wilmer just sent me his guy for home inspections. I'm going to call him now. In case we connect and schedule this, is there anything on your schedule this week that we need to plan around? As *you* know," Sawyer sarcastically says, "We only have a week to get the inspection done."

"Nope, I can pretty much go anytime this week."

After Sawyer gets off the phone, he says, "Got it scheduled. The inspector said I didn't have to be there. I find that weird. Do you think that's weird?"

"I don't think it's weird at all. Really just your personal preference, I guess," Hellen says.

***

On the day of the inspection, Hellen isn't feeling up to it. The pregnancy is continuing to wear her energy down easily and she wants to save it for her OB appointment later that afternoon.

"Ok, I'll meet you at the doctor this afternoon then."

"Ok. My appointment is at two. Good luck and I'll see you later. Love you, babe."

As Sawyer pulls up to the little yellow house, the sight of hooptie-ville across the street no longer bothers him. His doubts about the property are slipping away.

CHAPTER 9

The complete inspection took about an hour and Sawyer got most of his questions answered by Mr. Allan.

Discouraged by the home inspection, Sawyer plops into his smoldering hot car. The voices of all the people who told him to stay away from investing creep in, and self-doubt sets in like a monumental tsunami wave.

His thoughts are interrupted by his phone ringing.

"Hey, Atticus?"

"Hey, Sawyer. It's Atticus. Thinking about you and your deal, and I have some time this afternoon. Want to grab a drink?"

"Sure. Coincidentally I just finished the inspection. Are you free now?"

"Yes, sir. I'll meet you at the Brew & Hop in fifteen."

"See you then," says Sawyer as he hangs up and hits play on his most recent audiobook.

"Resistance. Resistance is invisible. Resistance cannot be seen, touched, heard, or smelled, but it can be felt. We experience it as an energy field radiating from a work in potential. It's a repelling force. It's negative. Its aim is to shove us away, distract us, prevent us from doing our work. Resistance is internal. Resistance seems to come from outside ourselves. We locate it in spouses, jobs, bosses, kids, peripheral opponents. Resistance is not a peripheral opponent. Resistance rises from within. It is self-generated and self-perpetuated. Resistance is the enemy within . . . Resistance will do anything to keep you from doing your work . . . If you take resistance at its word, you deserve everything you get. Resistance is always lying and always full of crap."

Sawyer pauses *The War of Art* by Steven Pressfield to exit his car and go in to meet Atticus.

Sawyer enjoys Atticus's company, and at times feels as if the real estate experience and mentorship he was receiving is an absolute bonus.

As Sawyer walks into the open-air establishment, the smell of fried hot wings combined with the fruit slushiness of a tropical bar and grill fills the air. The sound of Zac Brown "Unwinding" is heard on the overhead speakers and Sawyer spots Atticus sitting bar side, drink already in hand, talking things up with the bartender.

"Hey, Sawyer, saddle up here, bud." Atticus slaps the barstool next to him. "This here is Rick. He's taking care of this afternoon. Let him know what you want."

"I'll have one of those." Sawyer gestures to what Atticus is drinking.

"Good man. Make that two Rick," Atticus states as he flashes the peace sign.

"So, what's the plan? Already have a renter lined up? How did your inspection go?" Atticus takes another gulp.

"Already have a renter?" Sawyer scoffs then continues. "No, sir. This place needs some work before we can move anyone in."

"Don't let a little work persuade you from finding a good-paying tenant right away. The name of the game is positive cash flow, and you want to find a qualified renter as soon as possible. So, what all needs to be done?" Atticus pauses to take another large gulp.

CHAPTER 9

"Nothing big really. The bedroom needs new carpet, and—"

"Yep, that's typical for a turnover," says Atticus. "That should only be $400 to $500. What else?"

"Well, there is the carpet in the bedroom, but every wall in the place needs primer and a coat of paint, including the ceiling. And the kitchen and bathrooms need a severe deep clea—"

"Yea that doesn't sound too bad. Now, Sawyer, as long as you're approved, you're paying cash from your HELOC for this property, right?"

"Yes sir."

Rick returns with their drinks.

"Cheers, Sawyer." They clink bottles and take a drink.

"Well, it's a good idea to start gathering documents together and keeping them in an organized place. Banks can be your best friend but can also be the biggest pain in your ass. I know you're not dealing with a traditional loan on this one, but on the first one where you do, they're going to ask for all tons of shit. You'll think that you've given them everything except your firstborn to their precious underwriters and here they come again asking for more documentation. Do yourself a favor and start keeping a filing system for leases, rent rolls, your annual tax returns, insurance on your properties, your W2s. Put all that stuff in a place where you know you'll have it, and then when the time comes, you bring them your more recent bank statements, your personal financial statement, and pay stubs. It's a hell of a thing to deal with a bank. I'm glad I don't have to, and someday you won't have to either. When that day comes, and there is no more banko-pain-in-the-you-know-what-o, you know you've really made it.

"Well, the work to get this place ready doesn't sound bad at all. You should have that place ready in a week or two tops. Who do you have doing this work for you? And if that really is all the work it needs, you really need to be focused on finding you a qualified tenant."

"Yea, I don't have anybody lined up to do the work. I mean, I can paint and clean, and sure, I'll have to figure out how to do the carpet, but Hellen and I are going to do the work," Sawyer replies.

"What? You and your extremely pregnant wife are going to do the work?"

"That's right," says Sawyer. "Hellen won't be pregnant when we close, unless the baby is overdue, but the OB keeps telling us to keep a bag packed, and if anything, this baby is going to be early. We've already talked to our Realtor, and if we have to push the closing due to the pregnancy, the bank who holds the foreclosure is OK with that."

"Yeaaaa . . ." Atticus takes a sip and sits back in his chair. "Let me give you some advice, Sawyer. If there is ever anything I teach you, let this be it. This is your first kid, right? This one drafts you into dad status, right?"

"Yes, sir, that is correct."

Atticus lets out a light and amusing chuckle but continues. "Look, buddy, when people tell you that 'your world is about to change' when you have kids, those words are used because if the words existed to explain to you how much your world, and how much your and Hellen's lives are about to change by becoming new parents, you wouldn't believe them. I'm assuming you plan to paint and clean on the nights and weekends because you have to work during the day, correct?"

Atticus takes another sip. Sawyer nods yes, and Atticus continues. "Hopefully I can help you understand here. Your nights, Hellen's nights, ya'lls weekends are going to be spent cleaning a dirty bottom, taking naps, and trying to figure out how to sustain on just one to three hours of sleep per night. You're going to discover emotions that you didn't know existed and so will your wife. And you specifically on weekends are going to be with the child so your wife can sleep because she's been up all night with the baby and the baby needs to be fed again for the twelfth time today. You do realize that newborns eat about every two to three hours, right?"

"I do," Sawyer sprightly and confidentially replies as he sits up straighter in his chair with a "are you daring me I can't" grin.. "We got this. Hellen and I are committed to making this work, and we will. I have no doubt."

"I believe you will too, Sawyer. But the point I want to foster is positive cash flow is the name of the game, and the sooner you have a quality tenant in there, the better chance you have. Would you at least get some quotes from contractors to consider? I mean, sure, the experienced professional guys will cost you some money but the point being is they'll finish it quicker, making your property ready faster and cash flow, well, start flowing. Again, cash flow is the name of the game here."

"We already did get some estimates. That's why we're going to do the work ourselves."

"Damn, was the labor cost that much? What are we talking here?" Atticus motions for the check.

"Yea, it's pretty high. Labor alone was $1,500."

"Fifteen hundred bucks? That's all, are you kidding me?"

With doubt starting to set in, Sawyer swiftly responds, "Yea, well, from where I sit, that's a lot of money. Plus, if I'm not doing the work, then I'm managing someone who isn't going to do it to my standards, and I just don't think I'm going to find anyone to do that, so then I'm going to end up paying for a job that I'll eventually end up redoing myself."

Of course, these are all just excuses. Sawyer had no experience managing subcontractors and only read and heard about the horror stories.

"Alright, Sawyer, you seem to be dead set on attempting this yourself, with Hellen's help, of course. I think you're going to regret it in the end because you'll come out financially ahead by hiring subs to take care of this for you. You'll be able to get it rentable quicker so that your quality tenant can start paying you and Hellen that cash. Positive cash flow is the name of the game here, Sawyer, and the longer a property sits vacant or unable to rent, the longer it is before you'll see that cash flow. Look, I know when to cease beating a dead horse. Plus, I'm scheduled to view a property here in five minutes." Atticus stands up from the table.

"Oh shit, what time is it?" Sawyer checks his watch. He had been so intrigued with his conversation with Atticus he'd lost track of time. "Damn it, it's almost two. I'm supposed to meet Hellen at the OB at two, and it's twenty minutes away."

Atticus pats Sawyer on the back. Don't worry, Sawyer. Doctors are never on time. Let's just hope that baby is!"

Rustling to get his things together, Sawyer heads out the door.

***

YOUR NEXT STEPS TO MAKE AN OFFER:

- ☐ What to Expect from an Inspection: Inspections costs anywhere from $400–$1,000 for a single-family home and take one–two hours to complete. At a minimum, you will want to get a four-point (roof, HVAC, plumbing, and electrical) inspection. And if you live in states like Florida that require an extra wind mitigation report for insurance purposes, grab that too. If the property was built in 1978 or before, you may choose to have additional reports completed, but talk to your specific inspector about what to choose. And don't worry: an inspector is doing his job if he finds a ton of stuff wrong with the potential property you're buying. Do not let his report scare you away; rather, use it to renegotiate the price.
- ☐ Research Inspectors: Not all inspectors are created equal. I personally have had a time with ones I just found on the internet. The best ones come from referrals, so ask folks that you met in your REIA meetings and the people you've been meeting one on one with who they use for home inspections. Ask enough people, and you should hear a reoccurring name or entity. No need to reinvent the wheel here.
- ☐ Be Present for Your First Inspection: Now, you can't accomplish this until you have your first property under contract, but I want to bring it up here because I want to plant the seed and make the point that I want

you to attend the inspection, in person. You'll learn tons, and it doesn't take very long.

- ☐ Build a Rolodex of Handy People: You don't have to be handy! But you need to know people who are. Start building a Rolodex of subcontractors, tradesmen, and handymen. What I mean by this is you're going to need a handful of folks in your back pocket: property manager, plumber, electrician, HVAC, and roofer are the big ones. If you choose to hire a professional property manager chances are they have their own teams established, but you want to have your own to justify quotes and grab second opinions. Much like home inspectors, these subcontractors and tradesmen should come from referrals.
- ☐ Proceed to Chapter 10.

CHAPTER 10

GARAGE BAND

"Nothing stresses me out except having to seek the approval of my inferiors."

—Dwight K. Schrute

CHAPTER 10

Monday night, pizza night. Hellen is an amazing cook, and since they became newlyweds, Sawyer and Hellen learned they loved to cook together. Tonight wasn't filled with the dreary wearies. Sawyer had an uptick in his energy and overall positive attitude. Of course, *The Office* was playing on the set in the living room, muted, as the Zac Brown Band filled the air with "A Little Bit of Chicken Fried."

They navigate their small kitchen as if they are professional ballroom dancers. And when the artist approached lyrics they both knew, spatulas convert into microphones for the big duet.

"Alexa, volume 2," Hellen says. "Hey, Sawyer?"

"Yes, my love?"

"Insurance. Do we have insurance bound on the little yellow house yet?"

"Nope, we haven't closed on it yet. Don't we get insurance after we've bought the property?"

"No, you have to do it before. Remember when we bought this house and our Realtor called us about a week before we closed and asked us to send our insurance paperwork to the closing agent?"

"Oh, yea!" Sawyer gasps. "I do remember that now. I remember thinking why in the hell are we just hearing about this a week before. Turns out it was no big deal. Ah, the things you learn."

"So then is it OK with you if I start calling insurance companies tomorrow to grab quotes for the little yellow house?"

"That would be great!"

"Ok, I will get the insurance coverage to start on our closing date: October twenty-second. In the biz, they call this binding or when the policy is bound and active."

"In the biz?" Sawyer says with a grin, playfully mocking Hellen as he snags two cups to pour drinks for supper.

"Also, do you remember when we bought this house and our Realtor and banker kept telling us 'Don't make any big purchases until after we officially closed?'"

"Ummm, no I don't, but that's another great point. You are full of them tonight, hun. Well, that and another human being!" Sawyer's dad jokes were improving for the worse, and Hellen giggles to embrace them.

"I mean, we are buying the little yellow house on a HELOC, so I don't think any purchases or anything will affect our HELOC approval, right?" Sawyer says.

"Well, anything that can affect our credit could affect our HELOC approval. Things like big purchases and . . . "Hellen pauses.

"And what?" Sawyer playfully responds as his deep thoughts are replaced by confidence, assurance, and the best dance moves that could make anybody cringe.

"Ok, I don't know what you have going on over there," Hellen says as she points the melted mozzarella cheese dripping spatula in his direction. "But you do a great job of keeping our finances in order, making sure all of our bills get paid on time, and keeping our credit score at its best. Those are important things to help ensure our HELOC is approved. Right?"

CHAPTER 10

"Right, and thanks, babe." Sawyer, half winded, gives his best Axel Rose on stage sway impression.

Hellen continues, "Paying our bills on time really helps our credit stay stable and good, and that's a big factor with getting approved for this HELOC. You're working hard to create this for us so we can become real estate investors. Just keep doing whatever it is you're doing. It's working, and we are on our way to really making this happen, but you gotta quit doing . . . that"—she points to his spastic moves.

"Oh, you haven't even seen my best moves. I'm just getting started!"

"Uhh, I think I've seen plenty. If you don't quit, my water is going to break from all this laughing!"

"So have you seen this move yet?" Sawyer starts to two-step into the cotton-eye Joe. "No? Well, check this one out." Sawyer stops dancing. "Hey, have you heard the one about the pregnant couple who got approved for their home equity line of credit?"

"What?" questions Hellen as she slowly turns to Sawyer.

With raised eyebrows and a big smile on his face, he locks eyes with Hellen. "Oh, yea, babe. I got the call today, and I wanted to wait and surprise you. We're approved. We have a HELOC for $35,000!"

With a playful slap on her rear, Sawyer leans in, places his hand over Hellen's, raises the spatula, and pulls the microphone in to do his best Elvis impersonation: "Thank Ya, Thank ya very much."

"Now let's eat. This performance has me famished!"

***

YOUR NEXT STEPS TO MAKE AN OFFER:

- ☐ Find Proper Insurance: Not all insurance companies are the same, so shop around. Much like inspectors, tradesmen, subcontractors, and handymen, these should also come as a referral. If you're working with a Realtor, they should have a few for you to call. Also, the folks you've been meeting with one on one should have referrals for you as well. Call at least three insurance companies to grab a quote on your first deal and be sure to have the insurance policy bound for the closing date (this just means you're covered). Speaking of one-on-one meetings, time to meet with five new people.
- ☐ Who Do You Know: Talk to five more people this week about your ambitions to explore real estate investing, but this time meet them somewhere in the market you want to invest in and take a different route to the meeting location than you normally would. Again, ask them who they know that already invests and ask for that introduction. I am curious. Do you see a trend developing here?
- ☐ BONUS STEP: I mentioned this in Chapter 3, but it's worth repeating. If you currently own and have owned the house that you live in for a minimum of three years, start talking to your bank about pulling a home equity line of credit. It's best to have the HELOC in place and not have an immediate need for

those available funds versus having a property under contract and not having the funds to close.

- ☐ Proceed to Chapter 11.

CHAPTER 11

BIG NEWS DELIVERY

"Landlords grow rich in their sleep without working, risking or economizing."

—John Stuart Mill

CHAPTER 11

10:04 p.m. on Friday, September 7, Hellen and Sawyer head to the hospital, packed as if they are going to the beach for an entire month and don't plan on doing any laundry while they are gone. It is time for their scheduled induction. Hellen had been progressing with her pregnancy just fine, but some mild concerns expressed by her OB provided the perfect window for induced labor. They are not headed just to the hospital. Their destination within the next twenty-four hours is Parent Ville.

While at the hospital, they didn't have the most restful night, they soon would learn it was the most restful night they would have in a while. At 6:24 a.m., with three final painful, productive, and primal pushes, the sounds of a newborn baby crying fill the air. Hellen gasps in relief as tears start to race down her face. Sawyer's eyes fill up with water and his body rushes over with an emotion he had never felt before. Sawyer cries out, "IT'S A BOY!"

***

Three weeks later, feeling as restful as a new parent can be, Sawyer picks up his vibrating phone. It's 8:04 a.m.

"Hey, Sawyer. Real quick. Just want to ensure you have a certified check for tomorrow, and you have your insurance bound," says Wilmer.

"Certified check, yes. Insurance bound, got it."

"Alright, I'll see you at nine tomorrow morning. You know where the title company is right?"

"Yes, sir, over on 8th Ave. We'll see you at nine tomorrow."

"We? Ah cool. Is Hellen coming too?"

"Yes, sir, she and the little man. You'll get to meet Hunter."

"Oh man, how old is he now?"

"He turned three weeks yesterday."

"That's great. Alright, see you kids tomorrow." Wilmer hangs up.

"Who was that, babe?" whispers Hellen. She had just finished feeding Hunter, lain him down in his bassinet, and shimmed back under the covers to snooze.

"That was Wilmer. He was checking to ensure we have our certified check for tomorrow's closing, and we were good to go on insurance."

The next morning, as sleep-deprived as new parents could be, Sawyer woke before his alarm. Anxious was an understatement. Sawyer is so anxious he would have made coffee excited. Concerned, yes, but anxious.

He can no longer lie in bed. His nerves are getting the best of him, but knowing that Hellen caught less sleep that night because of Hunter, he lies still for as long as he could. What seems like an eternity is really only a few minutes.

"Get up before you explode," Sawyer whispers to himself. He quietly clasps his change of clothes, goes to the bathroom, and turns on the shower.

CHAPTER 11

As he turns off the shower and reaches for his towel through the shower curtain, he sees Hellen standing in front of the bathroom mirror, standing on her tip toes, hands reaching for the sky, with a big yawn on her face.

"Sorry. I didn't mean to wake you. My nerves are getting the best of me. I'm anxious. Are you sure we should go through with this?"

"Sawyer, if we back out now, what's the worst that could happen?"

"Well, we lose our $1,000 in earnest money for sure."

"And do YOU want that to happen?"

"Well of course not."

"So, where's the hesitation?"

"I don't know. Guess because we've never done this before . . ."

"Yep, but we've got this. Now dry your butt and get out so I can get in," Hellen says with a commanding yawn.

Regardless of any training, preparation, or experience in his resume or in anything in his life, Sawyer allows self-doubt to creep in. Confidence is killer and his lack of it was painful—whether it was negotiating a deal for work where he had the upper hand or asking Hellen to marry him. Moments just before "go-time" that little seed of self-doubt always inevitably slips in and exponentially starts to grow.

After he and Hellen exchange a light morning peck on the cheek and exchange places, Sawyer stands with a wet towel wrapped around his waist, looking at himself in the bathroom mirror. The steam from Hellen's hot shower begins to embrace his reflection. He can smell her sun-ripened raspberry shampoo. *Man, I love that smell.* He wipes the fog from the mirror with his hand. As he stands there, looking deep into his own eyes, taking a moment, he reflects on just how far they'd come in the past ten months: from the nerve-racking acquisition phone call from his now-former boss, through the acquisition, the painful customer visits, dealing with customers leaving, facing his fears to attend an in-person meetup, meeting with Atticus, spending late nights researching masterminds, creating their investing criteria, driving for dollars, having a baby, making an offer, going under contract, and working through the home inspection.

As the fog rolled in once again to cover up his reflection, Sawyer looks at himself one last time. *You got this, Sawyer Abernathy. Be the man that Hellen deserves. Be the father that Hunter deserves. Take a leap of faith in the process that you and Hellen have created. You. Got. This.*

"Hellen?"

"Yes, babe?"

"How's it coming in there?" he says jokingly.

Hellen responds in like gesture: "Oh, pretty good. How's it going out there?"

"Great. It's closing day!"

"Shhhhhh!!!" Hellen responds in a whisper louder than the falling water in the shower. "While I do love the sound of that babe, if you wake up Hunter, we're going to be late. I'm almost done in here, and it won't take me long to get ready."

CHAPTER 11

When they are ready to go, Sawyer picks up Hunter and takes him downstairs while Hellen finishes getting ready. Carefully placing Hunter in his car seat, Sawyer strikes up a conversation with him. "What's up, buddy? Today's a big day. It's closing day. You ready to become a real estate investor?"

Hunter blank stares up at him.

Self-doubt starts to creep back into Sawyer's thoughts. "Yea me too. It seems like you might be more ready than I am. We're doing this for you, buddy. Hope this is the right choice."

***

YOUR NEXT STEPS TO MAKE AN OFFER:

- ☐ Dealing with Self-Doubt: As a new investor, you're going to experience this a lot, at least I did. Did I run the numbers right? Did I evaluate the property correctly? This is where relying on the insight, motivation, encouragement, and push from experienced real estate investors comes in. You should be getting this from your one-on-one meetings, your local REIA, or from the members of the mastermind you joined. If you're not able to deal with your self-doubt, you need to improve your circle. Your circle is the five people you hang around the most. If those five people aren't encouraging you, pushing, and pulling you to get out of your comfort zone, then you need to replace them with someone who will. If you have yet to join a mastermind or want to check out the W2 Capitalist mastermind, go to **www.W2Capitalist.com/Mastermind** and apply.
- ☐ Circle Back to Your Why: At the end of Chapter 3 you went through the exercise of creating your why, the reason you want to invest in real estate. Write this down, post it up, move the post location frequently, and rely on your why when you're feeling discouraged.
- ☐ Find, Connect, and Interview Three More Realtors: Find and connect with three more Realtors that serve the area you identified in your invest-

ing criteria. The best Realtor will prove to be an invaluable resource during your investing journey, but you need to find them first. For a list of the questions you need to ask during your Realtor interviews, head over to **www.W2Capitalist.com/MakeAnOffer**. Once this task is completed and you've now interviewed six Realtors, continue your search until you find the right one that matches your style and is willing to represent you; not one that's just trying to get a transaction completed.

☐ Proceed to the final chapter, Chapter 12.

CHAPTER 12

WHAT'S THE BIG DEAL?

"Buy land, they're not making it anymore."

—Mark Twain

"Hun?" whispers Hellen as she stands in front of him, baby carrier and Hunter in hand.

"We need to go if we're going to be at the closing on time."

It is kind of early, Sawyer thinks as Hellen continues with her checklist: "Got the check? Have your driver's license? I have Hunter." She grins at her last statement. Hellen continues, "Today's a big day, isn't it? Are you ready?"

With that same grin Sawyer says, "Certified Check . . . check. Driver's license . . . check. Absolutely I'm ready. Let's go."

"8:32, right on time," Sawyer says sarcastically. His sarcasm was his defense mechanism at the building anxiety.

"We are ready," Hellen says.

A sudden rush of relief sweeps over Sawyer. Hellen's pre-planning to get them to the closing office early and the confident tone in her voice are all Sawyer needed. "Let's go," he replies.

The three of them, Sawyer and Hellen carrying Hunter, zip toward the entrance of the closing attorney's office. In Sawyer's mind, it is a sauntering amble with upbeat music. He is Wyatt Earp, and he and his men are on their way to disarm the red sash wearing cowboys from breaking the law at the OK Corral.

A bell rang as he opened the door. Being a gentleman, one who upholds the law of the Wild Wild West, he held the door open for Hellen. Wilmer is waiting for them in the lobby as everything played out full speed for Sawyer now. "Hey, you two, excuse me, you three," Wilmer says as he pokes his right index finger at a sound asleep Hunter. "Damn, didn't know he was sleeping."

"No worries. Hellen just set him up, so he should stay asleep for this entire thing," Sawyer replies as he reaches out to shake hands with Wilmer.

"Wow, you two look great. I was concerned this early of a closing that y'all would have trouble getting here. Can't imagine ya'll are sleeping much right now," says Wilmer.

"Well, one of us is sleeping just fine," Hellen says as she giggles and nods in Sawyer's direction.

"Ahhh, I get it. Did you bring your driver's license?"

"Yes, sir," says Sawyer.

"Go ahead and give them to Rebekah," orders Wilmer as he guides Sawyer toward the reception desk and continues, "They'll have to print copies of them, and we can go ahead and get that out of the way because they aren't quite ready for us to head to the conference room just yet."

Moments later, Wilmer, Hellen, Hunter, and Sawyer are escorted down a short hallway to a small conference room. "Can I get ya'll anything to drink?" asks Rebekah. Sawyer points to Hellen for her to respond first.

"I'm fine," Hellen replies.

"I'll take a water.," Sawyer's mouth is dry. He is slowly pacing the room as Wilmer takes a seat at the table.

Making her way around the conference table, Hellen sits Hunter's car seat carrier down on top of the table, near the end. She lifts the cover and peeks in on him. He hadn't moved. With a full belly and a clean diaper, he is good for a long nap.

Shortly thereafter Rebekah returns with Sawyer's water and behind her came Stephanie, the closing agent. "Alright, you guys ready to begin?" says Stephanie.

Minutes go by, document explanations are made, Sawyer's hand is cramping, and papers are sliding back and forth across the conference room table. "Sign here, and here, and here . . ." Swish, swoosh, swash. Swiftly, Sawyer moves through the merry-go-round of paperwork flying his way. He is becoming a signature ninja. The pen whips around like Bob Ross's paintbrush making a happy tree. Hellen is snapping pics and Hunter is sleeping away.

"Alright, we're done. Congrats you two, excuse me, you three. Y'all hang out in here while I go print copies of all this for you, and then you'll be on your way."

Hellen and Sawyer share a grin.

"Well, congrats kids," Wilmer says as he hands the keys over to Sawyer. "Let me take a pic of all three of you. This is a big day for y'all, and you'll definitely want the little man to have something to relive this memory by."

"Absolutely, thank you," Hellen chirps as she hands Wilmer her phone.

"Thanks, Wilmer, and we also want one with you in it."

"Everybody, say cheese!"

While heading back to their car, Sawyer says, "Well, what do we do now? I guess we need to head home, right He nods toward Hunter in his car seat carrier.

"Oh, we're fine and we're heading straight to our new house. We have to memorialize this, babe!" Hellen says as she clicks Hunter's car seat carrier in the back seat.

Sawyer sits silently for a moment, lost in thought, then finally speaks: "Well, I thought there would be more to it. I've been so anxious about this morning, I rarely slept last night. All the thoughts that have gone through my head up until that moment in there"—he points toward the window of the conference room— "everything up to this moment . . . if this was the climax, it was pretty . . . well . . . uneventful."

"That's what she said," Hellen chimes in using one of Sawyer's favorite lines to break the mood. "You mean to tell me, Mr. Sawyer Abernathy has been telling himself stories, worst-case scenario stories, and building up this giant monster in his head all this time?" Hellen lets out a loaded dish of sarcasm. "I'm sorry there wasn't a big scary dragon in there for you to slay for us, but, babe, you just did this for us. We've been searching for half a year for this opportunity, and you just made this happen. We are now real estate investors. Give yourself some credit and let's celebrate this moment!" She places her hand on the back of his neck, pulls him in tight. and kisses him on the lips as she continues, "I'm proud of you and Hunter's proud of you." After another smooch on the lips, she lets go of his neck, leans back in her seat, buckles her seat belt, and commands, "Now let's head to the little yellow house."

"You're right," Sawyer agrees. "Maybe this lack of feeling or unexpected lack of excitement is what Ziglar was referring to when he said, 'It's not a destination, it's a journey.' Huh, this is crazy stuff. We are real estate investors."

"So, is that what we're going to call it?" asks Sawyer.

"Call what? What do you mean?"

"Are we going to officially call it the little yellow house?"

With a flirty and excited grin, Hellen says, "I love it. Sounds great to me."

***

YOUR NEXT STEPS TO MAKE AN OFFER:

- ☐ Continue Your Education: As mentioned at the beginning of Chapter 1, Sawyer discovered audiobooks served a dual purpose. Continue your education by learning from those who have gone before you. Visit **www.W2Capitalist.com/BooksForBeginners** for a list of ten books I highly recommend for new investors.
- ☐ Enjoy the Process: Jumping over those emotional hurdles is a *big deal*, but once you get past them, you'll look back and laugh and wonder what the *big deal* was.
- ☐ Proceed to Make an Offer's Resource Website: Go to **www.W2Capitalist.com/MakeAnOffer** to grab all the resources, grab the bonus chapter, and join me for your free monthly Ask Me Anything session by registering at **www.W2Capitalist.com/MakeAnOffer**.
- ☐ Make an Offer: Yes, make an offer. If you haven't jumped ahead of the game by now, find a property that fits all of your criteria, and MAKE AN OFFER!

A SPECIAL INVITATION AND YOUR NEXT STEPS

"Since risk cannot be eliminated altogether the notion, we should avoid it at all costs is absurd. No, the goal should not be to remove risk but rather take calculated risks. What risk are you willing to take relative to the return you're hoping to receive?"

—Ryan Michler

Readers and listeners of *Make an Offer* find additional support and inspiration by being around like-minded individuals, from all over the country, who are on their own real estate investing journey. Some are just beginning to look at a map, while others have strapped on their boots and are trekking through the mountains. Regardless of where you are in your journey, I can guarantee that being around like-minded individuals will inspire, motivate, and propel you to overcome your next challenge. As a token of my appreciation for you purchasing this book, I want to specially invite you to join me for a free, *Ask Me Anything* session.

Register for the next session @ **www.W2Capitalist.com/MakeAnOffer**

Like Sawyer, once you are surrounded by the right people and influence, you will find the encouragement to not only make an offer on an opportunity that meets all of your criteria but also to successfully close on that criteria-meeting property and be on your way to building the type of portfolio you desire.

Through practice and repetition, you will build your market knowledge and your confidence to comfortably make offers on properties before visiting them or even performing a walk through.

Check out *The 10 Step Guide to Buying and Holding a Small Multifamily Rental Property* that allowed me to earn a 396 percent return on a duplex I owned for three years and never stepped foot inside. You can find this resource and all the book's resources at:

www.W2Capitalist.com/MakeAnOffer

THOUGHT PROVOKING QUOTES FOR THE ASPIRING REAL ESTATE INVESTOR

"Are you paralyzed with fear? That's a good sign. Fear is good. Like self-doubt, fear is an indicator. Fear tells us what we have to do. Remember our rule of thumb, the more scared we are of a work or calling, the more assured we can be that we have to do it."
—Steven Pressfield

"Kites rise highest against the wind, not with it."
—Winston Churchill

"In the manners of style, swim with the current. In the matters of principle, stand like a rock."
—Thomas Jefferson

"Efforts and courage are not enough without purpose and direction."
—John F. Kennedy

"Dream as if you'll live forever. Live like you'll die tomorrow."
—James Dean

"Sad will be the day for any man when he becomes contented with the thoughts he is thinking and deeds he is doing—where there is not forever the beating at the doors of his soul some great desire to do something larger; which he knows he was meant and made to do."
—Philips Brooks

ACKNOWLEDGEMENTS

(Last paragraph is to you)

To my friends who read the manuscript at different stages and never held back at providing their lighthearted but brutally transparent feedback, thank you.

To members of the W2 Capitalist Mastermind who contributed their emotional reminisce on their first deal and who constantly provide me with inspiration and motivation to spread this message, thank you.

To my editor, Katie Chambers, to my writing coach, Brett Hilker, to the Self-Publishing School Community, and to the entire launch team of Make an Offer, THANK YOU!

And to you, the reader, thank you. Thank you for purchasing this book and finding that motivation and encouragement to begin your real estate investing journey. Let's keep connecting on social media (you can find those links at **www.w2capitalist.com**). Please let me know how you're doing, what you're faced with, and if there is anything I can do for you. Act in the presence of fear, as the life you desire is just on the other side of your first deal. All right, now stop reading and start making offers!

ABOUT THE AUTHOR

Jay Helms is the author of *Make An Offer* and Founder of the W2 Capitalist. He spent nearly twenty years serving the Information Technology industry of Corporate America before he made a comfortable exit into full-time real estate investing entrepreneurship. With a mix of single-family- , small multifamily- , and apartment syndications in just six years of side hustling in real estate investing, he and his wife grew their portfolio to be financially independent while working a full-time job and bringing three beautiful kids into the world.

Being financially independent has allowed him to enjoy fun adventures with his wife, Cassie, whom he met when they were both contestants on a reality TV show, and his three kids, Rowland, Stella, and Ellen Anne. When they are not traveling the country in their RV, Jay and Cassie reside in Gulf Breeze, Florida.

Jay's goal is to help one million people create multiple streams of income, achieve financial freedom, or build legacy wealth through real estate investing.

Knowing that closing on the first deal is the biggest hurdle and roadblock for new investors, he wrote this book to help others get over those mental hurdles. Every investor faces paralysis analysis, but it is time to break through and make an offer.

Regardless of your reason to start investing, Jay and the W2 Capitalist Community want to help you create multiple streams of income, achieve financial independence, or build legacy wealth.

EARN. INVEST. REPEAT.

UNLEASH THE POWER OF MAKE AN OFFER TO YOUR REIA

ORDER BULK QUANTITIES

Order bulk quantities of this book to provide to your REIA or organization's members.

To find out more, email Jay at jay@w2capitalist.com

BRING THE AUTHOR INTO SPEAK

Bring Jay Helms in to speak at your next in-person or virtual REIA, team meeting, or conference.

MOST REQUESTED SPEAKING TOPICS:

- How To Balance a Full-Time Job, Growing Family, and REI Side Hustle
- How To Become a Successful Real Estate Investor
- Avoiding the Shiny Object Syndrome: How to Get Clear on Your Vision and Set SMART Goals

To Schedule Jay, email him at jay@w2capitalist.com

Made in the USA
Middletown, DE
27 July 2022

70079517R10096